VICTIM'S RIGHTS LAW

by
Margaret C. Jasper, Esq.

Oceana's Legal Almanac Series:
Law for the Layperson

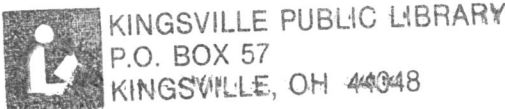
KINGSVILLE PUBLIC LIBRARY
P.O. BOX 57
KINGSVILLE, OH 44048

1997
Oceana Publications, Inc.
Dobbs Ferry, N.Y.

Information contained in this work has been obtained by Oceana Publications from sources believed to be reliable. However, neither the Publisher nor its authors guarantee the accuracy or completeness of any information published herein, and neither Oceana nor its authors shall be responsible for any errors, omissions or damages arising from the use of this information. This work is published with the understanding that Oceana and its authors are supplying information, but are not attempting to render legal or other professional services. If such services are required, the assistance of an appropriate professional should be sought.

You may order this or any other Oceana publications by visiting Oceana's website at http:\\www.oceanalaw.com

Jasper, Margaret C.
   Victim's rights law / by Margaret C. Jasper.
   p. cm. — (Oceana's legal almanac series. Law for the layperson, ISSN: 1075-7376)
   Includes bibliographical references.
   ISBN: 0-379-11241-8 (alk. paper)
   1. Victims of crimes—Legal status, laws, etc.—United States–Popular works. I. Title. II. Series.
KF9763.Z9J37   1997
344.73'03288—dc21

Copyright 1997 by Oceana Publications, Inc.

All rights reserved. No part of this publication may be reproduced or transmitted in any form or by any means, electronic or mechanical, including photocopy, recording, xerography, or any information storage and retrieval system, without permission in writing from the publisher.

Manufactured in the United States of America on acid-free paper.

To My Husband Chris

**Your love and support
are my motivation and inspiration**

—and—

In memory of my son, Jimmy

ABOUT THE AUTHOR

MARGARET C. JASPER is an attorney engaged in the general practice of law in South Salem, New York, concentrating in the areas of personal injury and entertainment law. Ms. Jasper holds a Juris Doctor degree from Pace University School of Law, White Plains, New York, is a member of the New York and Connecticut bars, and is certified to practice before the United States District Courts for the Southern and Eastern Districts of New York, and the United States Supreme Court.

Ms. Jasper has been appointed to the panel of arbitrators of the American Arbitration Association and the law guardian panel for the Family Court of the State of New York, and is a New York State licensed real estate broker and member of the Westchester County Board of Realtors, operating as Jasper Real Estate, in South Salem, New York.

Ms. Jasper is the author and general editor of the following legal almanacs: Juvenile Justice and Children's Law; Marriage and Divorce; Estate Planning; The Law of Contracts; The Law of Dispute Resolution; Law for the Small Business Owner; The Law of Personal Injury; Real Estate Law for the Homeowner and Broker; Everyday Legal Forms; Dictionary of Selected Legal Terms; The Law of Medical Malpractice; The Law of Product Liability; The Law of No-Fault Insurance; The Law of Immigration; The Law of Libel and Slander; The Law of Buying and Selling; Elder Law; The Right to Die; AIDS Law; Obscenity, Pornography and the Law; The Law of Child Custody; The Law of Debt Collection; Consumer Rights Law; Bankruptcy Law for the Individual Debtor; and Probate Law.

TABLE OF CONTENTS

INTRODUCTION xi
CHAPTER 1: THE VICTIM 1
   In General 1
   Reporting the Crime 1
   The Effects of Victimization 2
      Post-Traumatic Stress Disorder 2
         Physical Symptoms 3
         Psychological Symptoms 3
         Prognosis 4
         Incidence of Post-Traumatic Stress Disorder 5
      Secondary Victimization 5
   The Cost of Crime to the Crime Victim 5
   The Victims' Rights Movement 6
   Victim Assistance Organizations 6
   Victims' Rights Legislation 7
      In General 7
      Rights of Survivors of Murder Victims 7
      The Victim Impact Statement 8
      Specific Legislation 8
         Notoriety for Profit - Son of Sam Legislation 8
         Confidentiality 9
         Federal Victims Rights Legislation 10
            Title 42 U.S.C. §10606 - Rights of Crime Victims . 10
            Title 42 U.S.C. §10607 - Services to Victims 10
CHAPTER 2: THE CRIMINAL JUSTICE SYSTEM 13
   In General 13
   The Role of Law Enforcement 13
   The Role of the Prosecutor 14
   The Role of the Court 14
   The Role of the Corrections Department 14
      Probation 15
      Incarceration 15
      Parole 15
   The Role of the Victim 15
      In General 15
      Pursuing Civil Remedies 16

Victim Compensation and Restitution 17
  Compensation 17
    In General 17
    Eligibility 18
    Limitations on Eligibility 18
    Necessity of Proof 18
    Covered Expenses 19
    Surviving Family Members 19
    Medical Expenses and Burial Costs 19
    Financial Support 19
    Mental Health Resources 20
  Restitution 20
    Statutorily-Prescribed Restitution 20
    Eligibility 21
    Covered Expenses 21
    The Victims Justice Act of 1995 21
CHAPTER 3: VICTIMS OF SEXUAL ASSAULT 23
  In General 23
  Statistics 23
  Proof 23
  Legislation 24
    Megan's Law 24
  Services to Victims 24
  Confidentiality 25
  Rape-Related Post-Traumatic Stress Disorder 25
  Male Rape Victims 26
  Sexually Transmitted Disease 26
CHAPTER 4: VICTIMS OF DOMESTIC VIOLENCE 29
  In General 29
  Statistics 29
  Risk Factors 29
  Orders of Protection 30
  Strategies for the Domestic Violence Victim 30
    Strategies While Still in the Situation 31
    Making Plans to Leave the Situation 31
    Leaving the Situation 32

TABLE OF CONTENTS

CHAPTER 5: VICTIMIZATION OF CHILDREN	33
In General	33
Child Abuse and Neglect	33
Physical Abuse	33
Emotional Abuse	33
Sexual Abuse	33
Parental Child Abuse	34
Child Abuse - Strangers	34
Neglect	34
Child Pornography and Prostitution	35
Child Abuse Statistics	35
Child Protection Legislation	36
The Criminal Justice System	36
CHAPTER 6: VICTIMIZATION OF THE ELDERLY	37
In General	37
Statistics	37
Legislation	38
CHAPTER 7: VICTIMS OF HATE CRIMES	41
In General	41
Statistics	41
Legislation	41
Hate Groups	42
The Ku Klux Klan	43
Aryan White Supremacist Groups	43
CHAPTER 8: STALKING VICTIMS	45
In General	45
Statistics	45
Profile of a Stalker	45
Love Obsession Stalkers	45
Simple Obsession Stalkers	46
Legislation	47
Proof	47
Safety Strategies	47
APPENDIX 1 - STATE PSYCHOLOGICAL ASSOCIATIONS	51

APPENDIX 2 - RESOURCE DIRECTORY FOR
    VICTIMS—GENERAL 55
APPENDIX 3 - CRIMINAL JUSTICE RESOURCES 57
APPENDIX 4 - STATE VICTIM COMPENSATION
    PROGRAMS 59
APPENDIX 5 - ELIGIBLE PERSONS UNDER STATE
    VICTIM COMPENSATION STATUTES 63
APPENDIX 6 - COMPENSABLE CRIMES UNDER STATE
    VICTIM COMPENSATION STATUTES 67
APPENDIX 7 - MAXIMUM COMPENSATION
    AVAILABLE UNDER STATE VICTIM
    COMPENSATION STATUTES 73
APPENDIX 8 - THE VICTIMS JUSTICE ACT OF 1995 77
APPENDIX 9 - RESOURCE DIRECTORY FOR
    VICTIMS—WOMEN 85
APPENDIX 10 - RESOURCE DIRECTORY FOR
    VICTIMS—CHILDREN 87
APPENDIX 11 - RESOURCE DIRECTORY FOR
    VICTIMS—THE ELDERLY 89
APPENDIX 12 - RESOURCE DIRECTORY FOR
    VICTIMS—HATE CRIMES 91
GLOSSARY 93
BIBLIOGRAPHY AND SUGGESTED READING 105

INTRODUCTION

When a crime has been committed in the United States, it is considered to have been committed against society as a whole, rather than against the individual crime victim. Thus, the crime victim does not retain an attorney to bring the criminal action against the perpetrator. Instead, a public official—the prosecutor—brings the criminal action "on behalf of the people" of the particular jurisdiction where the crime was committed.

The victim's role in a criminal proceeding is basically reduced to that of a witness. The victim generally has little or no control over the proceedings or the outcome. As a result, the victim often feels helpless in the effort to achieve justice.

In large part due to this inability to participate in the system, a victims' rights movement has emerged over the past two decades, which seeks to give victims more input and control. This movement has been responsible for the passage of significant state and federal legislation concerning crime victims' rights.

In fact, every jurisdiction has enacted some type of crime victims' rights law, and at least twenty states have passed constitutional amendments to protect the crime victim, including Arkansas, Alaska, Arizona, California, Colorado, Florida, Idaho, Illinois, Kansas, Maryland, Michigan, Missouri, New Jersey, New Mexico, Ohio, Rhode Island, Texas, Utah, Washington and Wisconsin.

As crime statistics escalate, the public has become fully aware that crime affects every citizen of the United States. In addition to the usual crime statistics, certain crimes are targeted at specific populations, such as the elderly, children, minorities and women.

This legal almanac presents a general discussion of the criminal justice system, and the procedures a crime victim will likely encounter. This almanac further sets forth the rights afforded crime victims through growing legislation, and the resources available to crime victims in dealing with the aftereffects of victimization. In addition, crimes unique to specific populations are explored, including sexual assault, child abuse, domestic violence, stalking, hate crimes and crimes against the elderly.

The Appendix provides sample forms, applicable statutes, and other pertinent information and data. The Glossary contains definitions of many of the terms used throughout the almanac.

CHAPTER 1:

THE VICTIM

In General

A victim is generally defined as an individual who has suffered some type of loss or injury as a result of a crime. It is a sad reality that the majority of United States citizens have either been victims of crime, or know someone who has been victimized. According to FBI statistics for 1995, a violent crime occurred every 18 seconds, and there were 21,597 murders—one murder every 24 minutes.

In addition, persons 12 years old or older experienced 39.6 million crimes, approximately 9.9 million of which were violent crimes, such as rape, robbery and assault. Further, the Bureau of Justice estimates that, in 1995, 63% of crimes went unreported.

It is estimated that five out of six people will be the victims of a violent crime at least one time during their life.

In 1993, the cost of crime to the victims—e.g., the value of stolen property, lost wages, etc.—totalled almost twenty billion dollars, not considering other losses to the victim, such as pain and suffering and loss of enjoyment of life.

Reporting the Crime

It is important for the victim of a crime to immediately contact the law enforcement authorities. Crimes which are not reported cannot be investigated, and the perpetrators cannot be apprehended. Crimes which are not reported offer little deterrence to criminals who will most likely commit additional crimes until caught. Accurate crime statistics cannot be gathered if crimes go unreported, thus, communities in need of crime prevention resources will not receive adequate protection.

Further, if the crime victim fails to report the crime, they will not be entitled to compensation from the state's compensation fund. Most programs require that the victim report the crime within a certain time period after its occurrence. In addition, if recovery is sought from private insurance, the insurance company will likely require a copy of the police report. Also, it is unlikely that the victim will ever have stolen property returned to them if there is no record made of the theft with law enforcement authorities.

Unfortunately, a substantial number of crimes go unreported. There are a number of reasons why a victim may not report a crime. The most common reasons victims give for non-reporting include (i) fear of reprisal from the criminal; (ii) concern for privacy; (iii) inconvenience; (iv) relative insignificance of the crime; (v) lack of faith in the system; and (vi) lack of evidence.

The Effects of Victimization

Studies have concluded that victimization, particularly if the individual is victimized more than once, causes profound effects on the crime victim. Following a traumatic event, many people suffer what is commonly referred to as stress. Of course, being the victim of crime is quite a traumatic event for the victim and his or her family. This is particularly so if the crime was a violent crime.

Stress can be either long-term or short-term. A seriously destructive crime may cause stress in the victim's life for years following the event. Many people who suffer long-term stress are still able to function normally. However, when the stress interferes with one's ability to function, he or she may be suffering from a condition known as post-traumatic stress disorder (PTSD).

Of course, having experienced a traumatic crisis does not necessarily mean the victim will develop post-traumatic stress disorder. Victims who seek crisis intervention—e.g. counseling—early in the healing process have a much better chance of reducing the risk of developing post-traumatic stress disorder.

Post-Traumatic Stress Disorder

According to the Diagnostic and Statistical Manual of Mental Disorders, post-traumatic stress disorder occurs when a person has been exposed to an extreme traumatic stressor in which both of the following were present:

1. The person:

    (a) directly experienced an event or events that involved actual or threatened death or serious injury, or other threat to one's physical integrity; or

    (b) witnessed an event or events that involved death, injury, or a threat to the physical integrity of another person; or

    (c) learned about unexpected or violent death, serious harm, or threat of death or injury experienced by a family member or other close associate; and

2. The person's response to the event or events involve intense fear, helplessness or horror.

Post-traumatic stress disorder may affect the actual victim of the crime, as well as the victim's family and close friends, regardless of age or gender.

Post-traumatic stress disorder is defined as *acute* if it lasts for less than three months following the traumatic event. If it persists beyond that period of time, it is perceived to be a *chronic* condition.

There are a number of objective physical symptoms, and psychological symptoms which may indicate that an individual is suffering from post-traumatic stress disorder, as set forth below.

Physical Symptoms

Physical indicators of post-traumatic stress disorder include:

1. Irritability and the inability to control angry outbursts;

2. Inability to fall asleep and frequent awakening during sleep;

3. Inability to concentrate;

4. Easily startled and/or overly cautious.

Psychological Symptoms

Psychological indicators of post-traumatic stress disorder include:

1. Recurrent recollections of the event which cause severe distress, including flashbacks and illusions;

2. Recurrent stressful dreams replaying the traumatic event;

3. Intense psychological or physiological distress when exposed to internal or external stimuli which trigger thoughts or remembrances about the traumatic event, such as the anniversary date of the occurrence;

4. Avoidance of stimuli which are associated with the traumatic event;

5. A general numbness as indicated by attempts to avoid anything associated with the traumatic event, including thoughts, conversations, people, places or things which may trigger a remembrance of the traumatic event;

6. An inability to remember portions of the traumatic event, e.g. mental blocks.

7. Disinterest in activities and/or detachment from persons that formerly held importance in the individual's life;

8. A decrease in the ability to feel emotions experienced prior to the traumatic event;

9. A foreboding feeling about the future, e.g. focus on death or expectation of more traumatic experiences.

The avoidance of stimuli which trigger remembrance of the traumatic event, and the decrease in the ability to feel emotions, are symptoms commonly referred to as *psychic numbing*. These feelings usually appear soon after the traumatic experience as a defense mechanism in which the victim's mind virtually shuts out any stimuli which would cause the victim further trauma.

Post-traumatic stress disorder may affect all areas of a person's life—social, familial and occupational—and cause the individual an inability to function. The victim often experiences an intense range of emotions, from profound anger and sadness, to general numbness and withdrawal. This in turn could lead to divorce, job loss and other negative consequences stemming from the original traumatic event, as the victim's family, friends and co-workers attempt to cope with the individual's suffering.

Prognosis

The indicators of post-traumatic stress disorder may not manifest themselves until long after the traumatic event. If the symptoms occur six months or longer after the traumatic event, it is known as *delayed onset*.

Sometimes the victim may function normally for a period of time, and then some event, or a certain sound or smell, may trigger stress reactions, and cause the individual to have flashbacks, or relive certain aspects of the traumatic event. This phenomenon can occur from time to time for many years following the traumatic event, and may cause the individual to suffer physical symptoms, such as those associated with intense fear or panic.

Nevertheless, most victims eventually recover from post-traumatic stress disorder, and the severity of the symptoms decrease and disappear over time. Of course, the prognosis of recovery for each individual is dependent on a number of variables—e.g. severity of the crime—and some victims may suffer their entire lifetime.

One key factor in whether a victim will recover involves their ability to rebuild their lives and take control. If the trauma is confronted soon after it is experienced, the extent and duration of the psychological and emotional suffering is generally lessened, and the risk of even developing the stress disorder is significantly reduced.

A directory of state psychological associations is set forth in the Appendix.

Incidence of Post-Traumatic Stress Disorder

In 1977, a study was undertaken by the National Institute of Justice to determine the psychological impact of crime on victims. The individuals who took part in the study had been victims of crime an average of 15 years prior, and had not undergone any type of counseling.

According to the study, 28% of the crime victims subsequently developed crime-related post-traumatic stress disorder and 7.5% were still suffering from the disorder at the time of evaluation.

Secondary Victimization

A phenomenon known as *secondary victimization* refers to the aggravation of stress symptoms by those organizations which are in place to assist the victim, such as the criminal justice system, mental health resources; victim compensation programs, and the victim's family and friends; etc.

Secondary victimization often occurs when those working in the criminal justice system treat victims in an insensitive manner. The result is a second emotional trauma that can be more harmful than that caused by the original crime, and which serves to prolong the victim's stress disorder.

The Cost of Crime to the Crime Victim

Based on the 1992 statistics provided by the National Crime Victimization Survey, victims of crime suffered $17.6 billion dollars in crime-related costs, including lost wages, medical costs, property damage, and theft of property or money. The crimes involved included robbery, burglary, rape, assault, and stolen vehicles. The average economic loss totalled $524.

Approximately 31% of all crime victims in 1992 sustained some type of physical injury. For violent crimes resulting in injury in which medical expenses were known, 65% involved costs of $250 or more, and only 69% of those victims were covered by health insurance or receiving public benefits. Further, the 1.8 million crime victims surveyed lost a total of 6.1 million days from work.

Of course, the economic loss to crime victims continues to accrue long after the crime is committed. For example, medical costs, including psychological counseling expenses, are likely to continue for an undetermined period of time.

The Victims' Rights Movement

A victims' rights movement has emerged over the past two decades to champion the rights of crime victims. This movement has been responsible for the passage of important federal, state and local legislation designed to protect the crime victim and his or her family, permit the victim to participate more fully in the criminal proceedings, and provide valuable resources to the victim.

Victim Assistance Organizations

Crime victims often do not know where to turn for help in dealing with the emotional aftermath of the crime. This is particularly so if the crime victim decided, for whatever reason, not to report the crime to law enforcement officials. If the crime is reported, there are generally resources offered through the system. Information is usually provided by the prosecutor's office, the court, or the police department.

Many local communities offer programs to assist the victim, regardless of whether the crime is reported. Such programs are usually listed in the telephone directory under "victim's assistance." Victims of specific crimes may search under their particular category, e.g. "rape crisis lines"; "domestic violence lines", etc. In addition, assistance may be found by contacting local social services or mental health organizations.

Most victims assistance organizations provide a wide variety of programs, including therapy and counseling; support groups; and practical help and information. For example, assistance may be provided in obtaining compensation from state victim compensation boards, or in completing a victim impact statement.

A resource directory of organizations which assist crime victims is set forth in the Appendix.

Victims' Rights Legislation

In General

Specific legislation concerning victims' rights is further discussed below. In general, however, laws have been passed in all jurisdictions giving victims certain rights, sometimes referred to as the Victims' Bill of Rights." Some of the most important provisions of victims' rights legislation include:

1. The right to attend the criminal proceedings, including the trial, the sentencing, and any subsequent parole hearings, and the right to be heard;

2. The right to be notified of each stage of the criminal proceedings so that the victim can participate if he or she wishes to do so.

3. The right to compensation—such as that provided by state victim compensation programs—and restitution by the offender, including the right to recover compensation derived from the criminal's exploitation of the crime;

4. The right to be informed of all available legal remedies, including the right to pursue civil action against the criminal, e.g. to recover punitive damages; and

5. The right to be protected from harassment, including security during the criminal proceedings, and relocation assistance if warranted;.

Rights of the Survivors of Murder Victims

When a family member is murdered, the survivors' only recourse is to the criminal justice system to bring the criminal to justice, and thus provide the family with some closure to the tragedy. Historically, family members were not generally viewed as "victims of the crime," and they had little or no official involvement in the proceedings.

In recent years, this has begun to change, in large part due to the activism of the victims' rights movement. The victims' rights movement has fought to have the family of a homicide victim recognized as victims of the crime who are entitled to actively participate in the criminal proceedings. In fact, many states have enacted laws which consider crime victims to include family members of homicide victims for the purposes of affording them certain rights similar to those afforded the victim. These include the right to notification concerning the criminal proceedings; the right to be protected from harassment; the right to victim compensation and services; and the right to make a victim impact statement.

The Victim Impact Statement

A *victim impact statement* is a written or oral report which details the manner in which the crime affected the victim and the victim's family. The statement is commonly given at the time of sentencing, and at parole hearings at the time the criminal becomes eligible for parole.

The victim impact statement is usually offered by the victim, or the victim's survivors. In the case of a minor or incompetent victim, the statement may be offered by the parents or legal guardian of the victim.

The victim impact statement brings to the court's attention the pain and suffering caused by the crime, which may be expected to endure long after the criminal is sentenced. For example, the statement may describe the physical, mental or financial harm the crime has caused the family.

The victim impact statement also gives the victim and/or the victim's family, the chance to participate more fully in the criminal justice process and the quest to bring the criminal to justice. Many states even allow the victim to recommend a sentence or offer comments on the proposed sentence.

Most states have laws which give the victim and/or the victim's family, the right to make a victim impact statement, and require the court or the parole board to consider the statement when rendering a decision. The statement may also be contained in the criminal's presentencing report to the court, and periodically updated and sent to the parole board.

Specific Legislation

Notoriety for Profit - "Son of Sam" Laws

In 1977, New York enacted a statute known as the "Son of Sam" law. "Son of Sam" refers to David Berkowitz—a deranged serial killer who gripped New Yorkers with fear for a period of time during his murderous crime spree. Following his capture and conviction, David Berkowitz was presented with a number of lucrative offers to tell his bizarre story.

In response, New York enacted the "Son of Sam" statute which permits crime victims and their survivors to share in any profits derived from the sale of such a criminal's story. The reasoning for the "Son of Sam" law is to prevent criminals from profiting from their crimes while the victims continue to suffer, and are further subjected to additional exposure as a result of the publicity.

Following in New York's footsteps, the federal government and the majority of states enacted similar statutes. These laws generally provide that when a criminal contracts to receive profits from telling his or her story—e.g. a book or movie deal—the paying party is required to turn over any profits payable to the criminal directly to the state. These funds are then made available to the criminal's victims, and/or placed in the state's victim compensation fund.

Most states require the victim to sue the criminal and obtain a civil judgment for damages as a prerequisite for making a claim under the law. Other states rely on their victim compensation programs to handle the claims. The time limit for suing the criminal and making a claim varies among the jurisdictions. Therefore, the reader is advised to check the law of his or her own jurisdiction in this regard.

Since the enactment of the "Son of Sam" law, there have been constitutional challenges to the law. In 1991, in *Simon & Schuster vs. The New York Crime Victims Board,* The U.S. Supreme Court agreed and found that New York's law is overly broad and violates the constitutional right to free speech under the First Amendment. In response, the New York legislature enacted new legislation. Other states have also amended their "Son of Sam" laws to avoid being struck down as unconstitutional.

Confidentiality

Legislation exists in most jurisdictions which protects the victim's right to privacy, so as to encourage the reporting of crimes to law enforcement authorities and to protect the victim from secondary victimization by the media.

In particular, due to the nature of the crime, there are specific categories of crime victims entitled to confidentiality, including victims of rape and sexual assault, child victims, and victims of domestic violence. Laws may prohibit the release of the victim's name, address and telephone number, as well as the personal records of the victim, e.g. medical records. Some laws prohibit the media from publishing the victim's likeness or other identifying information, and in some states, those who do so may be liable for damages to the victim.

Federal Victims' Rights Legislation

Title 42 U.S.C. §10606 - Rights of Crime Victims

Section (b) of this statute affords the crime victim the following rights:

1. The right to be treated with fairness and with respect for the victim's dignity and privacy.

2. The right to be reasonably protected form the accused offender.

3. The right to be notified of court proceedings.

4. The right to be present at all public court proceedings related to the offense, unless the court determines that testimony by the victim would be materially affected if the victim heard other testimony at trial.

5. The right to confer with the attorney for the Government in the case.

6. The right to restitution.

7. The right to information about the conviction, sentencing, imprisonment, and release of the offender.

Further, Section 10606(a) requires that the employees of the Department of Justice and other Federal agencies engaged in the detection, investigation, or prosecution of crime, make their "best efforts" to see that crime victims are accorded the rights described above.

Title 42 U.S.C. §10607- Services to Victims

This statute requires that crime victims be informed of their right to receive the following services:

1. Emergency medical and social services;

2. The availability of restitution or other relief to which the victim may be entitled under law, and the manner in which such relief may be obtained;

3. Counseling, treatment and support through available public and private programs;

4. Assistance in contacting the persons who are responsible for providing the above-described services.

Further, the victim is entitled to protection from the suspected offender and any persons acting in concert with the offender.

This statute also states that, during the prosecution and trial phase of the proceedings, the crime victim is entitled to certain information, including notice concerning:

1. The status of the investigation of the crime, to the extent it is appropriate to inform the victim and to the extent that it will not interfere with the investigation;

2. The arrest of a suspected offender;

3. The filing of charges against a suspected offender;

4. The scheduling of each court proceeding that the witness is either required to attend or entitled to attend;

5. The release or detention status of an offender or suspected offender;

6. The acceptance of a plea of guilty or nolo contendere or the rendering of a verdict after trial; and

7. The sentence imposed on an offender, including the date on which the offender will be eligible for parole.

Following the trial and conviction of the offender, the victim is entitled to notice of any scheduled parole hearings, and notice of the offender's escape, work release, furlough, any other form of release from custody, or the death of the offender.

CHAPTER 2:

THE CRIMINAL JUSTICE SYSTEM

In General

The criminal justice system refers to the organizations and individuals involved in protecting society from crime, and bringing criminals to justice. The criminal justice process begins following the commission of a crime once it is reported to law enforcement authorities. Once an arrest is made, and charges are filed against the criminal, the crime is considered "a crime against the state."

The prosecuting attorney represents the interests of the state against the criminal, and only indirectly does he or she represent the interests of the victim. The goal of the criminal justice process is to adjudge the guilt or innocence of the accused. If he or she is found guilty, the criminal justice system is responsible for punishing and/or rehabilitating the criminal.

The crime victim, who has already been devastated by their misfortune, often confronts the criminal justice system with great apprehension, as they attempt to seek justice. It is therefore important that the crime victim develop a basic knowledge of the organizations that compose the criminal justice system, the individuals who are involved in the process, and the basic procedures followed in bringing an offender to justice .

A directory of criminal justice resources is set forth in the Appendix.

The criminal justice system can be broken down into four basic segments according to the role they play in apprehending, prosecuting and punishing the criminal, including (i) law enforcement; (ii) the prosecutor; (iii) the court; and (iv) corrections, as further discussed below.

The Role of Law Enforcement

Law enforcement officials generally make the first contact with the crime victim following the commission of the crime. It is the responsibility of the law enforcement official to investigate the crime, gather evidence, and apprehend and arrest the offender.

Once arrested, the criminal is usually taken by the law enforcement official to jail to be identified, fingerprinted and booked, and to await further processing. The law enforcement officer may also be responsible for conducting follow-up investigations, and to testify in the criminal proceedings.

If the victim witnessed the crime, he or she may be asked by the police to cooperate in the investigation. For example, the victim may be asked to try and identify the perpetrator. This may be accomplished by looking through books which contain photographs of criminals—known as "mug shots." In addition, the victim may be asked to view a lineup to see if he or she can identify the perpetrator in person. A lineup consists of a number of individuals who are viewed by the victim through a one-way mirror. The individuals may be asked to repeat certain words which were spoken during the commission of the crime. There are a number of other ways a victim may be asked to cooperate, such as wearing a "wire" to record incriminating conversations. Of course, such requests carry a certain amount of risk to the victim, and are not typically sought.

In any event, a victim is never forced to cooperate with law enforcement. However, as a practical matter, without such cooperation it is less likely that the crime will ever be solved and the criminal apprehended and brought to justice.

The Role of the Prosecutor

The prosecutor is responsible for representing the people of the jurisdiction in bringing the offender to justice. It is the prosecutor's decision whether or not to prosecute a particular case after reviewing all of the facts.

The prosecutor participates at every stage of the criminal proceedings, including the arraignment and bail determination, any preliminary hearings, the trial, and the sentencing phase.

The Role of the Court

The criminal proceedings are presided over by a criminal court judge, who is responsible for overseeing the proceedings, and making certain rulings. For example, the judge generally decides whether bail will be granted to the offender, and determines the acceptability of a plea bargain arrangement proposed by the prosecutor and defense attorney. In addition, the judge decides the offender's punishment, such as the sentence to be served.

The Role of the Corrections Department

After the criminal has been sentenced, it is the role of the corrections department to make sure that sentence is carried out. This may include supervision during a period of probation, incarceration or parole.

Probation

Probation refers to the period of time during which a convicted criminal must be supervised in lieu of incarceration, i.e., the sentence is suspended. Probation is usually awarded when the offender has little or no criminal history, and is not a danger to society.

An individual known as a probation officer is usually assigned to supervise the convict during his or her period of probation. The court may place certain conditions on the probation, such as the payment of certain fines, or participation in counseling. If the convict fails to comply with these conditions, probation may be revoked and the convict incarcerated for the remainder of the sentence.

Incarceration

If the convicted criminal is sentenced to a period of imprisonment, he or she is placed under the supervision of the prison staff. The prison staff is responsible for maintaining the security of the institution. The prison also provides the convict with educational opportunities, counseling, and job training, as well as medical care when required.

Parole

Parole refers to the period of time during which a convicted criminal must be supervised, upon release from prison after having served a portion of his or her sentence. The decision to parole the convict is made by the parole board after a hearing. The crime victim is entitled to attend the parole hearing, and to prepare a victim impact statement concerning his or her position concerning the convict's early release.

If parole is granted, the parole board generally places certain conditions upon the paroled convict. The convict is supervised in the community by an individual known as a parole officer. If the paroled convict violates the conditions of parole, he or she is returned to prison to serve the remainder of the original sentence.

The Role of the Victim

In General

Because the commission of a crime is considered to be an act committed against society, the crime victim is not considered a party to the criminal proceeding. The state basically takes the role as the plaintiff, and the state's attorney prosecutes the case against the criminal—the defendant.

The victim has very little input into the criminal proceeding. He or she cannot force the government to prosecute the criminal if the prosecutor determines that there is not enough evidence. Of course, as further set forth below, the crime victim is entitled to bring a civil action against the criminal to recover damages, and the victim is also entitled under most state laws, to receive compensation from some type of victims' compensation fund.

In the context of the criminal proceeding, the victim's role is basically that of a witness to the crime. The victimization forms the basis for the criminal prosecution of the "social wrong." However, the victim does not have a right to assume any control over the criminal proceedings.

As set forth in Chapter 1, the victim does however have certain basic rights connected with the proceeding, e.g. the right to be present at all stages of the prosecution, and the right to protection from intimidation. In addition, the victim has the right to present a victim impact statement on various occasions—e.g. at sentencing or parole hearings—for the court or parole board to consider when rendering a decision concerning the criminal.

Pursuing Civil Remedies

The civil justice system, unlike the criminal justice process, does not rule on the guilt or innocence of the criminal, nor does it subject him or her to criminal penalties, such as incarceration. The goal of the civil justice system is to determine whether the criminal—referred to as the defendant—is civilly liable for the injuries caused by the crime. If the defendant is found to be liable, he or she is generally required to pay monetary damages to the victim or the victim's survivors. In order to be held liable, the standard of proof is that the defendant be found liable by a preponderance of the evidence. This is a much lower standard than required in a criminal case. Thus, even if the defendant is never prosecuted criminally, or is acquitted in the criminal court, the victim is still permitted to bring a civil action against the defendant.

A crime victim has the right to pursue civil remedies against a criminal for the losses and injuries sustained as a result of the crime committed. Although, as stated above, a criminal conviction is not required in order for a victim to pursue civil remedies, the fact of a conviction in criminal court can be powerful evidence of the criminal's liability in the civil action.

Unfortunately, it is often the case that the criminal is judgment proof, i.e., he or she does not have any financial resources or assets against which a monetary judgment can be enforced. Nevertheless, civil actions have been successfully prosecuted against third parties who may be held jointly responsible for the acts of the criminal, and who do have resources against which a judgment can be satisfied.

For example, if an employer negligently hires an individual who commits a crime during the course of his or her employment, the employer may be held responsible. Another scenario in which a third party could be held responsible occurs if a building owner does not provide adequate security for the tenants. If a crime is committed as a result of the inadequate security, the building owner may be held responsible.

By taking civil action, victims are able to recover monetary damages for such items as pain and suffering, medical expenses, lost wages, and property loss. Nevertheless, winning a monetary judgment does not guarantee payment. Many criminals are judgment proof. The victim is more likely to collect on the judgment from those third parties found responsible through their negligent actions.

Victim Compensation and Restitution

Compensation

Victim compensation refers to the money paid to a crime victim through state victim assistance programs. Such monies are paid out to try and compensate the crime victim for some of his or her pecuniary losses as a result of the crime.

Although financial relief cannot heal the trauma associated with victimization, it does serve to relieve the victim of further upset associated with monetary pressures, such as loss of income, payment of medical expenses, etc., which can prove devastating.

All of the states and the District of Columbia have established, by statute, some type of victim compensation program. There has not yet been established any similar federal compensation program, although the state programs are often partially federally funded.

A directory of state victim compensation programs is set forth in the Appendix.

Eligibility

While specific relief may vary, most victim assistance programs are similarly constructed. Of course, the crime victim is the primary recipient of the compensation. This is so whether or not the offender is ever apprehended provided the crime victim follows all of the procedural requirements.

In addition, many states also provide compensation to certain family members of homicide victims—known as secondary or derivative victims—as further discussed below.

A table of persons eligible under state victim compensation statutes is set forth in the Appendix.

The application for compensation must be made within a certain time period following the crime—e.g. two years—in the state where the crime took place. The governing law would also be the state where the crime took place, even if the victim's home state would provide greater compensation.

The types of crimes which are compensable vary among the states. Serious offenses, such as felonies, are usually covered by the statutes. A list of compensable crimes under state victim compensation statutes is set forth in the Appendix.

Limitations on Eligibility

Depending on the specific circumstances surrounding the crime, most states have placed limitations on eligibility. Although state statutes may vary, the most common situations in which a primary or secondary victim would be denied compensation benefits are set forth below.

1. A victim who was involved in the commission of a crime at the time he or she was victimized is not eligible for compensation.

2. Victims who do not cooperate with law enforcement officials in the criminal proceedings are not entitled to compensation.

3. Victims who do not meet a state-mandated financial needs test are not entitled to compensation.

4. Victims who have had their expenses covered by other sources, such as insurance coverage, are not entitled to duplicate compensation.

Necessity of Proof

Most statutes require the victims to provide proof of their losses, such as medical bills, funeral bills, and proof of lost income, before they will compensate the victim. The victim must have reported the crime to law enforcement authorities, usually within 24 to 48 hours of its occurrence. Nevertheless, there is no requirement that the criminal be convicted, or that he or she is ever arrested for the crime.

Covered Expenses

Most statutes provide compensation to the victim for the items listed below, up to a statutory maximum amount:

1. Lost wages;

2. Medical Bills;

3. Funeral Expenses;

4. Financial support for dependent family members of a homicide victim; and

5. Necessary psychological treatment and counseling.

A small minority of states will compensate victims for their "pain and suffering." Most victims are directed to file a civil lawsuit against the offender or any negligent third parties to recover monetary damages for pain and suffering.

Surviving Family Members

Many state victim compensation programs provide financial assistance to the family members of homicide victims. Such compensation may include any financial losses or expenses which resulted from the death of the victim, as set forth below.

Medical Expenses and Burial Costs

The following states have enacted specific legislation which compensates surviving family members for the crime victim's medical expenses and burial costs: Colorado, Hawaii, Illinois, Massachusetts, Missouri, Nevada, New York, Texas and West Virginia.

Financial Support

The following states have enacted specific legislation which provides for financial support of the crime victim's surviving financially dependent family members: Arkansas, Connecticut, Florida, Georgia, Hawaii, Illinois, Indiana, Kentucky, Maryland, Michigan, Minnesota, Nebraska, Nevada, New

Hampshire, New York, Oregon, Pennsylvania, Rhode Island, South Carolina, South Dakota, Tennessee, Utah, Virginia, Washington, Wisconsin and West Virginia.

Mental Health Resources

The following states have enacted specific legislation which compensates certain surviving family members for the cost of psychological counseling related to the trauma of their loss: California, Idaho, Iowa, Massachusetts, Mississippi, Montana, Nevada, New York, Pennsylvania, Tennessee and Texas.

In addition, the court may order the offender to provide restitution to the surviving family members for any financial losses they suffered as a result of the loss of their loved one. However, these statutes do not generally provide the right to punitive damages. Thus, the family members must pursue a civil action for wrongful death to recover such damages, as further discussed above.

A table setting forth the maximum compensation available under state victim compensation statutes is set forth in the Appendix.

Restitution

Restitution refers to the requirement that the individual who caused harm to the victim must repay the victim. Restitution differs from compensation in several respects. First, the offender must be convicted of the crime for the court to take any type of punitive measures. Restitution must be made by the criminal, who more than likely does not have the resources to pay the victim.

In the past, restitution has largely been ignored as an appropriate remedy, in favor of focusing on punishing the criminal. In large part due to the emergence of the victims' rights movement, restitution has once again been recognized as an invaluable method to hold the offender accountable for his or her crime.

Statutorily-Prescribed Restitution

There has always existed a common law right to require restitution from one who has caused harm as a result of a crime. Most states have now enacted legislation which allows for restitution, and many courts now use restitution as a condition of probation. Failure of the criminal to make restitution can result in the revocation of his or her probation. Many states also require restitution and, in cases where restitution is not ordered, those states require the court to state its reasons for not doing so.

Eligibility

Of course, restitution can only be ordered if the offender is apprehended and convicted, unlike victim compensation which can be applied for whether or not the criminal is ever caught. All primary victims of a crime are eligible for restitution. Many states also permit the surviving family members of a homicide victim to recover for the cost associated with the victim's loss, such as medical expenses and funeral costs.

Covered Expenses

Most statutes provide restitution to the victim for the items listed below, which may include:

1. Out-of-pocket costs such as medical expenses and the cost of psychological counseling;

2. The cost of property damage; and

3. Lost wages.

The Court generally specifies the amount of the restitution to be paid, and the manner of payment. However, if the defendant is not able to pay, the court may not be permitted to order more than what would be reasonable considering the offender's financial resources. If the offender does not comply with the restitution order, he or she may be subject to incarceration, and if the offender is on probation, his or her probation may be revoked.

The Victims Justice Act of 1995

The Victims Justice Act is a restitution statute introduced by Representative Bill McCollum (Florida) on Jan. 25, 1995. As of April 10, 1996, differing versions had passed the House and Senate. The differences are being resolved by conference committees.

The Victims Justice Act would require that victims of federal crimes be awarded restitution in most cases. The version of the bill as passed by the Senate is set forth in the Appendix.

CHAPTER 3:

VICTIMS OF SEXUAL ASSAULT

In General

Sexual assault is a general term which refers to a number of sex-related offenses, including rape, sexual contact, and indecent exposure. The crime of sexual assault almost always involves sexual intercourse, including oral or anal intercourse, or some other type of penetration of the genitals. Penetration may be by another's body or by an object. Sexual assault involves the commission of those acts against another who is either unwilling to consent, or who lacks the physical, mental or legal capacity to consent, e.g. a minor.

Statistics

According to the Bureau of Justice Statistics, in 1995, victims reported an estimated 260,310 completed or attempted rapes and 94,580 sexual assaults. The Federal Bureau of Investigation further reports that, in 1995, one forcible rape occurred every five minutes.

The profile of the most likely victim of rape or sexual assault is a female, between the ages of 16 and 19, who lives in an urban center and comes from a low income household. Although the victims of sexual assault are primarily female, many states have recently amended their laws to make such crimes gender-neutral.

Proof

In prosecuting a sexual assault case, the issue of consent is of primary importance. If the victim was acquainted with the offender—e.g. date rape—it often becomes a matter of credibility unless there is further corroborating evidence, such as witnesses. However, some states have passed laws prohibiting law enforcement officers from requiring the victim of a sexual assault to submit to a polygraph test as a condition of beginning the criminal investigation.

In addition, most states no longer require evidence that the victim attempted to physically resist the attacker, and in all 50 states, it is now a crime to sexually assault one's spouse.

The defense usually attempts to undermine the victim's credibility by exploring the victim's sexual history and reputation. It is because of this embarrassment that the majority of sexual assaults go unreported to police.

Legislation

Over the last two decades, many states have passed laws to reform the procedures for prosecuting sexual assault so that permissible evidence focuses on the specific facts of the alleged assault, rather than the victim's past sexual conduct. In fact, most states have passed legislation—"rape shield" laws —which prohibits the introduction of the victim's past sexual history into evidence.

Usually, a preliminary hearing will be held before trial to determine if any evidence concerning past sexual conduct by the victim is relevant to establishing the facts of the case.

Megan's Law

Over 40 states have passed laws requiring the registration of sexual offenders with state agencies. This type of law has commonly been referred to as "Megan's Law" named after a child who was sexually assaulted and murdered by a convicted sexual offender, who was living in her neighborhood in anonymity.

The law basically requires that neighbors, community officials, organizations and individuals working with potential victims, such as children, or those likely to come in contact with the offender be notified that a convicted sex offender is living amongst them. Registration is required in order to keep track of the behavior and whereabouts of sexual offenders.

Services to Victims

There has been a growing need for services to victims of sexual assault for which funding has been sought. The types of services to victims that may be funded are:

Medical examinations unrelated to evidence gathering;

Ongoing medical treatment;

Onetime or ongoing sexually transmitted disease testing;

Psychological counseling and treatment;

Replacement of clothing;

Moving expenses; and

Other services or assistance.

Confidentiality

Many states have enacted laws which protect any conversations between sexual assault victims and their counselors. The purpose of the confidentiality statutes is to permit the victim to recover without fear that her identity will be uncovered to the public and/or the criminal.

Rape-Related Post-Traumatic Stress Disorder (RR-PTSD)

According to the National Victim Center, nearly one-third of all rape victims develop what is known as Rape-related Post-traumatic Stress Disorder (RR-PTSD) at some point in their life following the attack.

The first symptom of RR-PTSD is the feeling of reliving the traumatic experience. This occurs when the victim is unable to block out remembrances—e.g. flashbacks—about the rape incident. There are often accompanying nightmares in which the victim relives the whole experience. In addition, the victim often feels overwhelming distress when confronted with stimuli which symbolize the trauma.

Another major symptom of RR-PTSD is social withdrawal, also referred to as "psychogenic numbing," which leaves the victim feeling emotionally dead. The victim no longer experiences normal feelings such as those felt prior to the traumatic incident. For example, victims may no longer feel the normal range of human emotions, such as happiness and sorrow. Survivors of crime victims may also experience a decreased interest in living.

The victim is also likely to develop a form of amnesia concerning the details of the experience. This is a defense mechanism which takes over to protect the victim from experiencing further psychic trauma.

A third major symptom of RR-PTSD involves avoidance behavior. Avoidance behavior occurs when the victim attempts to avoid any thoughts, feelings or contacts which might stimulate a remembrance of the trauma. For example, a rape victim may refuse to drive in the area close to where the sexual assault occurred.

The fourth set of symptoms includes an exaggerated startle response, inability to sleep, memory impairment, and difficulty concentrating. Victims may also exhibit episodes of anger and irritability which have no identifiable cause. Rape victims are three times more likely to suffer major depressive episodes as compared to those who have not been victimized. In addition, rape victims are 4.1 times more likely to contemplate suicide, and thirteen percent actually follow through with a suicide attempt. Some also develop drug and alcohol problems following the traumatic experience.

Male Rape Victims

According to the Bureau of Justice Statistics, approximately 60,000 rapes of males age 12 and over occurred in the United States in 1992. The perpetrators of these crimes were primarily other males. Many experts also believe that these statistics are very low compared to the actual number of such rapes which occur each year. As further set forth below, male rape is a much more underreported crime than female sexual assault.

In the past, the subject of male rape has not received a lot of attention, in large part due to prevailing attitudes about sex, in general. Little research has been conducted on this subject, and the effects of these crimes on the victims. Nevertheless, because studies have concluded that sexual assault is borne of aggression, and not motivated by sexual desire, this would suggest that the gender or age of the victim may in some cases be irrelevant.

The research that has been undertaken concerning the psychological effects of rape on male victims demonstrates that males experience similar reactions, including depression, anger, and guilt. Males also experience sexual dysfunction and a damaged self-image following such an attack.

Because of prevailing attitudes, males are even more reluctant to report the crime than female rape victims. It is a fact that society generally believes that men should be able to protect themselves and are more at fault for allowing a rape to take place. Thus, there is less sympathy for the male victim, who does not receive the emotional support given his female counterpart.

One of the biggest reasons males fail to report rape is their fear of being identified as a homosexual. This is so even though, as stated earlier, sexual assault is an act of aggression, power and control, and the sexual orientation of the perpetrator and/or the victim is largely irrelevant. The fact is that male rape is a violent crime that affects heterosexual men as well as homosexual men.

In fact, knowledge of the male's reluctance to report a sexual assault is so common that criminals have been known to rape their male victims merely because they know that this will deter the victim from reporting the crime. In addition, the commission of hate crimes against homosexuals ironically often includes incidents of forcible rape accompanied by verbal harassment and other forms of violent assault.

Sexually Transmitted Disease

An additional factor in the psychological trauma associated with sexual assault is the fear that the victim has been exposed to a sexually transmitted disease and, in particular, to the potentially deadly and widespread HIV infection.

According to statistics gathered by the Center for Disease Control (CDC) in 1994, there had been 441,528 documented cases of AIDS, of which 270,870 infected individuals have already died. The CDC estimates that by the year 2000, approximately 100 million adults and 10 million children will be infected worldwide.

The incidence of HIV infection is so pervasive that most citizens know of at least one infected person. It is no wonder that victims of sexual assault are concerned about potential exposure. The fear is real and greatly exacerbates the stress a victim of sexual assault is already caused to endure.

Following the assault, the victim must make the decision on whether to be tested. It is recommended that the victim receive counseling both before and after being tested. If they wish to be tested, it is important that the test be taken as soon after the assault as possible for a baseline reading.

If the test results are negative, it is suggested that additional testing take place every six months for the following eighteen months. Of course, if the test results are positive, the impact will be devastating and intensive counseling will be required.

Nevertheless, the victim should be aware that a positive HIV test does not mean he or she has, or will develop, full-blown AIDS. Further, medical treatment has advanced to the point where death is not imminent, and some HIV infected individuals experience little, if any, symptoms.

A more detailed discussion of this topic may be found in this author's legal almanac entitled AIDS Law (1996), also published by Oceana Publishing Company.

CHAPTER 4:

VICTIMS OF DOMESTIC VIOLENCE

In General

Domestic violence refers to violence which occurs in the home, among family members. Family members may include spouses and former spouses, children, unmarried couples, and other relatives. In general, all states have laws which prohibit physical abuse, including sexual assault, and emotional abuse. However, in the past, law enforcement authorities were reluctant to get involved in domestic disputes. Due to the increasing number and severity of domestic violence incidents, police have begun to take a more active role.

For example, police frequently arrest an abuser if they have reason to believe that physical violence has taken place. In some states, if police fail to arrest an offender, they must provide a written report explaining their reasons for failing to effectuate an arrest. Police are also called upon to enforce orders of protection which typically require an abusive mate to stay away from the victim's residence. Further, police are usually responsible for arranging the transport of domestic violence victims to appropriate medical facilities and/or a shelter.

Statistics

Research demonstrates that women are more at risk for being victims of domestic violence than their male counterparts. It is estimated that 6 million women are assaulted by their husbands or male companions every year, a significant number of which are considered to involve severe injuries. According to the Federal Bureau of Investigation, in 1993, 29% of female murder victims were killed by their husbands, former husbands, or boyfriends. In this same time period, only 3% of male victims were killed by their wives, former wives, or girlfriends.

An individual convicted of murdering their spouse generally receives a less severe sentence than one who commits murder against non-family members. In fact, one study showed that approximately 90% of spouse murderers receive an average prison sentence of 13 years.

Risk Factors

Research has indicated a number of identifying factors which place a man at risk as a potential batterer, including: (i) unemployment; (ii) poverty;

(iii) drug or alcohol use; (iv) witnessed spousal abuse among parents; (v) uneducated; (vi) 18 to 30 years of age.

A recent study suggests that possessiveness was the most prevalent reason given by male offenders for killing their partners, and spousal homicide occurs more frequently during a period when the couple are separated, particularly if the separation was initiated by the wife.

Orders of Protection

A domestic violence victim is often advised to obtain an order of protection. An order of protection in a domestic relationship is usually obtained by filing a petition with the Family Court of the jurisdiction where the victim lives. An order of protection is issued on either a temporary or permanent basis.

The court will likely issue a temporary order of protection, upon the filing of the petition, based on the victim's allegations that she is in imminent danger of physical harm. The abuser is entitled to answer the allegations contained in the petition for an order of protection. If it is determined that the allegations are true, a permanent order of protection will be issued. The maximum length of time an order of protection may last varies according to state law.

A typical order of protection may (i) prohibit the abuser from contacting the victim; (ii) prohibit the abuser from further abusing or harassing the victim; (iii) require the abuser to provide support to the victim and children; and/or (iv) require counseling.

After a victim has obtained an order of protection, she can call the police if the abuser violates it. In some states, police are required to arrest the abuser if there appears to be a violation, e.g. the abuser is found outside the victim's home.

Unfortunately, statistics have shown that no piece of paper can completely protect a domestic violence victim from an abuser who is intent on causing physical harm. As of 1993, all states and the District of Columbia had passed "stalking" laws in an attempt to protect victims, usually women, who are followed, harassed, and threatened by their former mates. The matter of stalking is further discussed in Chapter 8 of this almanac.

Strategies for the Domestic Violence Victim

The following information has been gathered from nationwide domestic violence organizations, such as the National Victim Center, in order to give the domestic violence victim some strategies at various stages of a domestic violence relationship.

Strategies While Still in the Situation

Of course, a victim of domestic violence is advised to immediately leave the situation to avoid serious personal injury to herself or the children. Nevertheless, it is recognized that many women, for whatever reason, try to endure the violent behavior for as long as possible. In those cases, the following tips should be considered:

1. If it appears that abuse is about to occur, don't be combative. Try to diffuse the situation by backing down or leaving the situation to allow your partner to cool off.

2. Prepare safety areas in your home where you can go if you must escape abuse. If an abusive situation appears imminent, go to that area. Try to have a phone in that area in case you need to call for help. Maintain and try to remember a list of important phone numbers, such as the police, ambulance and shelter. Keep all types of weapons, if any, locked up in a remote location.

3. If you have children, try to stay away from them during an abusive episode so that they do not also become targets of the abuser.

4. If you are unable to avoid the violent attack, protect vulnerable areas of your body,—e.g. your head and face—by blocking with your arms.

5. Don't hide your situation from family and close friends. You may have to rely on them for help if the situation gets really out of hand.

6. Teach your children how to get help if the need arises. Caution them not to involve themselves in the altercation. Explain to them that violence is wrong, and they are not at fault.

Making Plans to Leave the Situation

If the situation becomes too turbulent and unpredictable to endure, the domestic violence victim must make plans to leave the situation. In that case, the following tips should be followed.

1. You should maintain a journal of all of the violent incidents, and keep it and any evidence of physical abuse, such as photographs, in a safe place where you will have access to them after you leave.

2. If you are injured, seek medical care at the emergency room of a hospital or your physician. Make sure your account of the injuries is documented.

3. Contact your local battered women's shelter for information about your legal rights, sources of financial assistance, counseling and other available resources.

4. If you are unemployed, seek out job training and educational programs to help prepare you for entering the workforce.

5. Practice an escape plan in case the need arises. Plan for all possible contingencies. For example, get into the habit of having your car ready for emergency departures and a spare set of keys in case yours are confiscated. Hide some emergency money, and keep a suitcase packed with some essential clothing and supplies for yourself and your children.

Leaving the Situation

1. Ask the police to accompany you while you remove your personal belongings from the home and escort you from the home.

2. Make sure you take with you important items that you will need and may not want to risk reentering the home to retrieve, such as your drivers license; legal documents, such as your marriage license, birth certificates, citizenship documents and social security cards; banking information and checkbook; property ownership documents, such as titles and deeds; credit cards; medical records and prescription medication; school records; insurance information; personal valuables and effects; and your personal telephone book with important phone numbers.

3. Try to create a false trail so that the abuser cannot easily track you down. Don't use calling card numbers that can be traced back to your whereabouts. Don't use credit cards in areas that you intend to relocate.

After you successfully leave the violent relationship, seek advice from domestic violence organizations on how to proceed to protect yourself and your children from further abuse. Court intervention may be necessary. In extreme cases, relocation may be the only alternative.

A resource directory of organizations specifically focused on the needs of women crime victims is set forth in the Appendix.

CHAPTER 5:

VICTIMIZATION OF CHILDREN

In General

It is a sad fact that children are often the innocent victims of crimes perpetrated against them by both family members and strangers. Crimes against children include (i) child abuse and neglect; (ii) emotional abuse; and (iii) sexual abuse, including introduction to the deviant world of child pornography.

Child Abuse and Neglect

Physical Abuse

The Child Abuse Prevention Treatment Act defines physical abuse as "inflicting physical injury by punching, beating, kicking, biting, burning, or otherwise harming a child." Such injuries may have been unintentional, e.g. having resulted from excessive physical punishment.

Emotional Abuse

It is often the case that a child's emotional well-being is ignored provided that he or she appears to be physically well cared for. However, the reality is that emotional abuse of a child often carries much deeper and longlasting scars than a physical beating. Some examples of emotional abuse which negatively impair a child's psychological health include: (i) constant verbal assault on the child; (ii) rejection; (iii) punishment involving close confinement; and (iv) the threat of physical harm. Children who have suffered psychological mistreatment are often characterized by low self-esteem and aggressive or other socially inappropriate behavior.

Studies have shown that parents who suffered emotional neglect as children often repeat this behavior with their own children. Drug and alcohol addiction, a stressful home environment and the mental state of the parent are also known to contribute to this problem.

Sexual Abuse

Child sexual abuse has been defined by the U.S. Department of Health and Human Services to include "fondling a child's genitals, intercourse, incest, rape, sodomy, exhibitionism and the sexual exploitation of a child."

The child victims of sexual exploitation and sexual abuse, in general, come from a wide variety of family backgrounds, including all socioeconomic classes and religions. They range in age from infancy through adolescence. Young children are often victimized by someone they know, e.g. a neighbor or family member. Many crave adult affection, and are lured into the behavior to obtain approval by adult authority figures.

The long-term effects on children who have been victims of sexual abuse are devastating. They are generally unable to form normal sexual relationships with persons of the opposite sex. Many child victims fall into destructive lifestyles, such as drug and alcohol addiction, and many succumb to suicide.

Parental Child Abuse

Studies have shown that parents who suffered abuse as children often repeat this behavior with their own children. Further, parents who suffer from drug or alcohol addiction are more likely to abuse their children. Abuse has also been found to exist to a greater degree when the home environment is under stress, e.g. a single-parent household, or a household suffering from depressed financial conditions, etc.

Child Abuse - Strangers

There is an increased awareness of the potential for child abuse to occur in institutional settings, such as schools or day care centers. As a result, most states require the employer to conduct a criminal history background check of employees and license applicants employed in child care facilities and other institutions.

Many of these laws allow only for a check of the convictions in a person's record, but others also include a check for prior arrests, and whether the applicant is known by the state's sex offender registry.

Neglect

The Child Abuse Prevention Treatment Act defines child neglect as "the failure to provide the child's basic needs." This would include physical, educational or emotional needs. For example, neglect would include the failure to seek necessary health care for a sick child, or the failure to enroll a school-age child in an educational program. The factors which indicate the likelihood of physical abuse in a particular household are substantially the same for child neglect.

Child Pornography and Prostitution

Child pornography and prostitution are highly organized, multi-million dollar industries that operate in our society on a nationwide scale. In 1977, Congressional hearings were held on the subject of child pornography, also known as "kiddie porn." Witnesses who appeared before Congress told nightmare tales about small children who were kidnapped by pornographers, or sold to pornographers by their parents.

Outraged federal and state legislators have since attempted to enact laws to combat this widespread problem. Following the 1977 Congressional hearings, two federal statutes were passed. First enacted was *The Protection of Children from Sexual Exploitation Act of 1977* which prohibits the production of any sexually explicit material using a child under the age of sixteen, if such material is destined for, or has already traveled in interstate commerce.

In response to allegations that children were being sold by their parents into the pornography industry, the law was made applicable to parents or other custodians who knowingly permit a child to participate in the production of sexually explicit material.

Subsequently, greater enforcement was obtained by enacting *The Child Protection Act of 1984* which eliminated the requirement that child pornography distribution be undertaken for the purpose of "sale," and raised the age of protection to eighteen. In addition, penalties under the 1984 Act were greatly increased over those set forth in the 1977 Act, and a provision for criminal and civil forfeiture was included.

Child Abuse Statistics

In 1994, approximately 3,140,000 children in the United States were reported to Child Protective Services as victims of child abuse or neglect. Of that number, approximately 1,300 children died as a result.

The factors within a family setting which contributed to this high incidence of abuse and neglect included (i) drug and/or alcohol abuse; (ii) poverty; (iii) lack of education; (iv) lack of parenting skills; (v) broken families; and (vi) domestic abuse.

Studies show that girls are three times more likely to be sexually abused than boys, however, boys are more likely to suffer serious injury or death as a result. A large study of female adults found that sexual abuse of girls generally began at age 6 and lasted approximately 7 years. The perpetrator in more than half of those cases was the child's own biological father. Boys, however, are more likely to be abused by males outside of the family.

Child Protection Legislation

Most state statutes provide privacy protection for child victims by requiring confidentiality concerning the identity of the child. In addition, many states prohibit the release of information relating to child abuse reports and investigation records.

In an effort to combat child abduction, most states have adopted laws relating to missing children. For example, many states now require that a missing child's school records and birth certificate be flagged in some way. Schools often require a child's birth certificate and/or prior school records in order to register the child. Thus, if the abductor tries to register the child, and requests these records, the school will be alerted to the whereabouts of the missing child.

Child protection laws are continuing to change, as states seek to find the most effective means to protect children from victimization. As discussed in Chapter 3, in response to the brutal sexual assault and murder of a little girl at the hands of a convicted sex offender who moved into the neighborhood, "Megan's Law" was enacted. "Megan's Law" requires the registration of a convicted sex offender, and notification to a community that he or she has moved into the neighborhood.

The Criminal Justice System

The awareness that a child must be treated with sensitivity and care has led to efforts to make a child's participation in the criminal justice system less traumatic. As a result, special rules generally apply when a child is a witness in a criminal case, particularly when there is a potential for emotional trauma.

These include (i) the use of a child's videotaped witness statements and/or closed circuit testimony rather than live testimony in front of the perpetrator; (ii) conducting proceedings in a closed courtroom; (iii) permitting testimony to take place in the judge's chambers; and (iv) limiting the amount of time a child is required to testify without taking a break.

A resource directory of organizations specifically focused on the needs of child crime victims is set forth in the Appendix.

CHAPTER 6:

VICTIMIZATION OF THE ELDERLY

In General

Older people have often been targeted as victims of crime, largely due to their frailty and inability to adequately defend themselves. However, as the baby boom generation moves towards senior citizenship, this group constitutes a much larger segment of society, and thus draws more attention than ever before. In addition, senior citizens represent a powerful political block which politicians can no longer ignore. In response, more effective legislation is being enacted to protect the elderly.

Due to their relative inability to protect themselves, the elderly are subjected to types of crimes which prey upon their weaknesses. For example, the elderly are particularly susceptible to crimes motivated by financial gain, such as muggings, robberies, and burglaries.

There is a growing phenomenon—"domestic elder abuse"—which refers to crimes against the elderly committed by family members or caregivers, and which generally occurs within the victim's home. This abuse often takes place at the hands of spouses and adult children. It is reported that alcohol consumption is a substantial factor in the abuse. In these scenarios, the majority of the abusers as well as victims are female.

Statistics

According to the 1994 Bureau of Justice Statistics, persons age 65 or older are the least likely group to be victimized. Nevertheless, state reports have shown a dramatic increase of 206% in elder abuse and neglect since 1987.

The elderly are particularly vulnerable to crimes involving financial gain as compared to younger victims. For example, robbery constitutes 38% of the violent crimes against the elderly versus only 20% of the violence experienced by persons younger than age 65. Elderly victims of robbery and theft are more likely than younger victims to report those crimes to law enforcement officials.

The elderly are much more likely to be victimized at or near their home. This is due to the fact that many senior citizens live alone, are unemployed, and spend most of their time in their homes or the immediate neighborhood. Consequently, fear of leaving their home, particularly after dark, is a common concern among senior citizens.

Elderly victims are vulnerable, and are less likely to act in their own defense than younger victims. Older victims generally do not take any type of physical action against their perpetrator, and are less likely to resist. In addition, elderly men generally have higher victimization rates than elderly women although elderly women are more susceptible to personal thefts, such as muggings and purse snatchings.

The typical, —and most susceptible—elderly victim has the following characteristics:

1. Age range of 65 to 74
2. Minority
3. Urban center resident
4. Separated or divorced
5. Apartment dweller

Further, the elderly in lower income brackets experience higher violence rates, and elderly in higher income brackets experience more economic crimes.

Legislation

In an effort to deter crimes against elderly victims, and to express society's intolerance toward such behavior, many state legislatures have created special classes of offenses involving crimes against the elderly. Many states provide that crimes committed against the elderly carry harsher penalties.

In addition, federal and state legislation is being passed which provides special protection and privileges to elderly victims of crime. For example, most crime victim compensation statutes require a minimum loss—e.g. $100—to be eligible for relief. Due to the realization that many senior citizens survive on fixed incomes, this minimum loss requirement is generally waived for the elderly victim.

Further, legislators have enacted mandatory reporting requirements concerning elder abuse which requires certain designated mandatory reporters—such as health care providers—to report suspected elder abuse or neglect. The reporter is required to report the incident or risk penalty for failure to report.

States have also enacted laws to deal with the special needs of elderly victims who must participate in the criminal justice system. For example, crimes involving elderly victims often receive a trial preference, i.e., priority scheduling on the trial calendar. In addition, some states permit an elderly victim to testify by alternate methods—e.g., by videotape or closed circuit television—as opposed to coming into court. Further, being mindful of diminished visual and auditory senses, most states accommodate elderly victims by providing enlarged visuals and sound amplification devices.

A resource directory of organizations specifically focused on the needs of elderly crime victims is set forth in the Appendix.

CHAPTER 7:

VICTIMS OF HATE CRIMES

In General

Hate crimes—i.e, violence motivated by a prejudice against an individual's race, ethnicity, religion, gender or sexual orientation—are a serious threat to our society. Individuals who commit hate crimes harbor animosity and negative views towards one or more groups of people who share common characteristics.

We are not born hating certain groups of people. Such hatred is usually perpetuated by an individual's upbringing and social contacts, and rooted in ignorance. Most prejudiced individuals have no true knowledge about the people they dislike. They are influenced by other sources, including the biased portrayal of certain groups by the media, e.g. television programs and movies. They are often isolated from these groups and rely on such portrayals, along with their social conditioning, to form their own incorrect beliefs about certain groups of people, as a whole.

Most hate crimes involve assault and battery, harassment and/or vandalism, and can be particularly violent. These acts are akin to terrorism, because they are designed to create fear in the victims.

Statistics

According to the Federal Bureau of Investigation, there were 1,947 reports of bias-related incidents in 1995. Of course, this figure does not take into account the vast number of bias-related incidents that go unreported. Victims of hate crimes are often reluctant to come forward for fear that they will be re-victimized by the criminal justice system. Some studies estimate that a hate crime is committed every 14 minutes in America.

According to the 1995 FBI statistics, the number of hate crimes according to group identification included: (i) Anti-Black (3,945); (ii) Anti-White (1,554); (iii) Anti-Jewish (1,236); and (iv) Anti-Male Homosexual (937). In addition, the acts of violence were broken down into the following categories: (i) Intimidation (4,048); (ii) Simple Assault (1,796); (iii) Aggravated Assault (1,268); (iv) Murder (20); and (v) Forcible Rape.

Legislation

Because of the unique harms caused by bias-related violence, special legislation has been enacted in many states. The reason that hate crimes need special legislation is the recognition that the state has a compelling interest in protecting society from violence motivated by prejudice.

Such violence, although largely committed against individuals, is in reality committed against an entire community of persons, and ultimately against society as a whole. Hate crimes cause Americans to become suspicious and fearful of their neighbors, and creates tension in communities. Hate crimes often spawn more violence, and may lead to retaliation, resulting in a continuous vicious cycle that must be broken. Thus, to protect the peace and order of the country, it is necessary to swiftly and harshly address bias-related violence so that a clear message is sent that such behavior will not be tolerated in a just society.

Anti-bias legislation is opposed by some groups on constitutional grounds, expressing concerns over freedom of speech. In response, the U.S. Supreme Court has recently ruled that although "hate speech" cannot be banned, states have the right to punish conduct motivated by such hate.

Hate crime legislation is critical in the effort to demonstrate society's intolerance of bias-related violence. Further, hate crime legislation protects the right of an individual to be free from this type of random, senseless violence, and deters bias-related crime by severely punishing such behavior.

As of 1992, the Federal government, 47 states and the District of Columbia all had some type of hate crimes statute. Many of these laws define the type of incident which qualifies as a "hate crime" and assess a greater penalty when the behavior is motivated by prejudice. For example, such laws might differentiate between a simple assault as opposed to an assault which is motivated by racial hatred, the latter receiving a harsher punishment.

Hate crime legislation generally requires that statistics be kept regarding the occurrence of bias-related incidents in order to effectively root out and deal with the problem. The federal Hate Crimes Statistics Act of 1990 established a national system for collecting bias crime statistics. The reasoning for this law is to bring greater public attention to the alarming rise in hate crimes, and to more effectively prosecute such crimes.

Hate Groups

As of 1992, there were over 300 known "hate groups" in the United States, with membership exceeding 20,000 individuals. In addition, many more citizens follow and support these groups in some way. The most infamous of these hate groups is the "Ku Klux Klan," and the "Aryan" groups, all of which have as their common theme the belief in white supremacy.

The Ku Klux Klan

The Ku Klux Klan is perhaps the most well known of all hate groups. The Ku Klux Klan emerged following the Civil War. The White south attributed the destruction of the southern states' economy to the abolition of slavery. The Ku Klux Klan committed numerous acts of violence, including murder, to create fear in southern Blacks, and stop their efforts to exercise any rights.

Out of anger and frustration, many individuals either joined the Ku Klux Klan, or supported the group's activities affirmatively or by non-opposition. Their hatred spread to include other groups, such as Catholics, Jews and immigrants. By 1925, the Ku Klux Klan had a membership exceeding five million Americans.

During the civil rights movement of the 1950's and 1960's, the Ku Klux Klan responded with brutal acts of violence, including murder, bombings and arson. However, because of active criminal and civil prosecution of the Ku Klux Klan, particularly by groups such as the Southern Poverty Law Center as part of their Klanwatch project, membership in the Ku Klux Klan has since dwindled. Nevertheless, there has been no shortage of hate groups ready and willing to take their place and promote bias-related hatred and violence.

Aryan White Supremacist Groups

There are a number of hate groups that surfaced in the late 1980's and early 1990's, many of which use the term "Aryan" in their titles, e.g. "The White Aryan Resistance," "The Aryan Youth Movement," "Aryan Independence", and "Aryan Nations."

The Aryans were prehistoric people from Northern Europe who spoke Indo-European. The term "Aryan" as used by these hate groups commonly refers to Caucasian gentiles, and is derived from Nazi ideology that the Aryans are a superior race of people.

These so-called Aryan groups espouse these white supremacy views, and promote violence against non-whites, particularly the Jews. They believe that they are the true descendants of Adam and Eve and that all other peoples represent evil.

The Aryan groups heed the racist beliefs of mass-murderer Adolf Hitler. They have recruited youths to join in their hate mongering—commonly known as "skinheads"—and have used these youth groups to advance and perpetuate their racist views.

A resource directory of organizations specifically focused on the needs of hate crime victims is set forth in the Appendix. The Hate Crime Hotline is 1-800-347-HATE.

CHAPTER 8:

STALKING VICTIMS

In General

The term "stalking" describes any unwanted contact by an individual—referred to as a "stalker"—and his or her victim, which places the victim in fear for his or her safety. However, the legal definition of stalking varies according to state law, which may specifically define prohibited stalking behavior.

The act of stalking is not new. It is essentially conduct which was previously described as a form of harassment. Only recently has stalking been categorized as a separate offense, in large part due to the number of celebrity victims who have been subjected to stalking.

Statistics

Mandatory tracking of stalking crimes went into effect with the passage of the 1994 Crime Bill, therefore, preliminary statistics are not particularly reliable. However, it is estimated that approximately 200,000 citizens are currently being stalked, and that 1 in 20 women will be stalked at least one time during their life.

Profile of a Stalker

Although most stalkers are male, a stalker can be any gender. A stalking victim can be either male or female, however, most victims are female. Stalkers come from all types of backgrounds. Because this phenomenon has only recently been subjected to scientific study, clearcut psychological profiles have not yet been determined. However, forensic psychologists generally place stalkers in one of two broad categories: (i) Love Obsession Stalkers; and (ii) Simple Obsession Stalkers.

Love Obsession Stalkers

A love obsession stalker is one who becomes fixated on an individual with whom they have no relationship, e.g. a total stranger or someone who they barely know. The stalkers who stalk celebrities fall into this category, which accounts for approximately one-fourth of all stalking behavior.

Psychologists believe that most love obsession stalkers suffer from schizophrenia or paranoia which is manifested in delusional thoughts and behavior. Their inability to function normally in relationships causes them to create a fantasy life in which their victim plays an important role as their love interest. They then proceed to try and live out this fantasy life.

Of course, the victims are unaware of their role in this obsession, and are unwilling to participate. In turn, this causes the stalker concern as he or she tries to make the victim conform to his or her role. The stalker may resort to threats, intimidation, and even violence, so that their fantasy can be brought to fruition.

Simple Obsession Stalkers

A simple obsession stalker is one who is obsessed with an individual with whom they had a previous personal relationship. This category makes up the majority of stalking behavior. The simple obsession stalker is commonly an ex-husband or mate who desires to control his former partner. "Fatal attraction" stalkers—individuals who become obsessed during a casual short-term relationship—also fall under this category.

Simple obsession stalkers generally do not have a mental disorder as do love obsession stalkers, however, psychologists do believe these individuals suffer serious personality disorders, similar to those exhibited by physical abusers in domestic violence situations.

The characteristics which appear to be common to all simple obsession stalkers, include: (i) the inability to maintain relationships; (ii) extreme jealousy and possessiveness; (iii) emotional immaturity and insecurity; (iv) low self-esteem; and (v) the need to control their partners through intimidation and/or violence.

Thus, once their partner leaves, this rejection causes their self-esteem to plummet as they become paranoid about their loss of control over that person. They become obsessed with regaining possession and total control over their former mate. If they are unable to do so, they often resort to violence—e.g., "if I can't have him/her, nobody else will." In fact, there is a very high incidence of spousal murder associated with domestic violence victims who decide to leave their partners.

Nevertheless, the behavior of stalkers is often unpredictable. That is what makes the crime so dangerous. The perpetrator may be sending love letters and roses one day, and the following day physically assault the object of their obsession. Conversely, the stalker may engage in non-threatening stalking behavior for many, many months without ever escalating to a more aggressive stage.

Legislation

In 1990, California became the first state to pass a law which specifically defined stalking as a crime. This action was taken in response to several cases in which stalking victims were eventually murdered. These victims had previously tried to make complaints to the police about the stalking behavior, however, the existing law required that the offender take some affirmative action before they could make an arrest. This requirement was changed with the new stalking law, permitting police to intervene at an earlier stage.

All 50 states subsequently enacted some type of anti-stalking legislation. Although the specific provisions may vary state by state, they all generally prohibit stalking behaviors that are intimidating and place the victim in fear for his or her safety. In addition, a number of criminal justice and victims' rights organizations have since promulgated a model stalking statute, and a recently enacted federal law prohibits an individual from crossing state lines for the purposes of stalking his or her victim.

The reader is advised to check the law of his or her own jurisdiction for specific provisions of that state's stalking law.

Proof

Although stalking laws no longer require the victim to wait until the stalker takes some affirmative action, the victim is still required to provide sufficient evidence to establish probable cause that the perpetrator engaged in illegal conduct. The victim is advised to keep a journal documenting each stalking incident. Photographs and videotapes, voice mail messages, correspondence and witness affidavits are types of evidence that may be used to establish probable cause.

Safety Strategies

A stalking victim who is being subjected to particularly threatening behavior should go to the nearest police station and immediately report the crime. If it is not possible to find a nearby police station at the time, safety may be sought at a church, shelter or other public place where a stalker is less likely to make a scene. Until the situation is brought under control, the stalking victim may consider relocating to a location where he or she will not be found.

If the danger is not imminent, but the potential for violence is there, a stalking victim should consider petitioning the court for an order of protection, as discussed in Chapter 4 of this almanac. Again, however, the reader is cautioned that an order of protection is merely a piece of paper, and will not stop a perpetrator who is intent on harming his or her victim.

APPENDICES

APPENDIX 1:

STATE PSYCHOLOGICAL ASSOCIATIONS

STATE	ADDRESS	TELEPHONE NUMBER
Alabama Psychological Association	P.O. Box 97, Montgomery, AL 36101-0097	205-262-8245
Alaska Psychological Association	P.O. Box 241292, Anchorage, AK 99524	907-696-8921
Arkansas Psychological Association	Three Financial Center, 900 S. Shackleford, Suite 300, Little Rock, AR 72211	501-228-5550
Arizona Psychological Association	6210 E. Thomas Rd., Suite 209, Scottsdale, AZ 85251	602-675-9477
California Psychological Association	1010 Eleventh Street, Suite 202, Sacramento, CA 95814-3807	916-325-9786
Colorado Psychological Association	1660 S. Albion, Suite 712, Denver, CO 80222	303-692-9303
Connecticut Psychological Association	50 Founders Plaza, Suite 107, East Hartford, CT 06108	203-528-8550
District of Columbia Psychological Association	750 First Street N.E., Suite 5127, Washington, DC 20002-4241	202-336-5557
Delaware Psychological Association	P.O. Box 718, Claymont, DE 19703-0718	302-475-1574
Florida Psychological Association	408 Office Plaza, Tallahassee, FL 32301-2757	904-656-2222
Georgia Psychological Association	1800 Peachtree Street N.W., Suite 525, Atlanta, GA 30309	404-351-9555
Hawaii Psychological Association	P.O. Box 10456, Honolulu, HI 96816-0456	808-377-5992
Iowa Psychological Association	P.O. Box 320, Knoxville, IA 50138-0320	515-828-8845
Idaho Psychological Association	1365 North Orchard, Suite 316, Boise, ID 83706	208-376-2273

STATE	ADDRESS	TELEPHONE NUMBER
Illinois Psychological Association	203 N. Wabash, Suite 910, Chicago, IL 60601-2413	312-372-7610
Indiana Psychological Association	55 Monument Circle, Suite 700, Indianapolis, IN 46204	317-686-5348
Kansas Psychological Association	400 S.W. Croix, Topeka, KS 66611-2251	913-267-7435
Kentucky Psychological Association	120 Sears Avenue, Suite 202, Louisville, KY 40207-5063	502-894-0777
Louisiana Psychological Association	P.O. Box 66924, Baton Rouge, LA 70896-6924	504-344-8839
Maine Psychological Association	12 Spruce Street, Box 5435, Augusta, ME 04330	207-621-0732
Maryland Psychological Association	1 Mall North, Suite 314, 10025 Governor Warfield Parkway, Columbia, MD 21044	410-992-4258
Massachusetts Psychological Association	14 Beacon Street, Suite 714, Boston, MA 02108-3741	617-523-6320
Michigan Psychological Association	24350 Orchard Lake Rd., Suite 105, Farmington, MI 48336	810-473-9070
Minnesota Psychological Association	1740 Rice Street, Suite 220, St. Paul, MN 55113-6811	612-489-2964
Missouri Psychological Association	410 Madison St., Jefferson City, MO 65101-2989	314-634-8852
Mississippi Psychological Association	P.O. Box 1120, 812 N. President Street, Jackson, MS 39215-1120	601-353-1672
Montana Psychological Association	P.O. Box 6367, Helena, MT 59604-6367	406-227-5292
Nebraska Psychological Association	1044 H Street, Lincoln, NE 68508-3169	402-475-0709
Nevada Psychological Association	3601 Skyline Blvd., Suite 35, Reno, NV 89509	702-827-6944
New Hampshire Psychological Association	P.O. Box 1205, Concord, NH 03301	603-225-9925

STATE PSYCHOLOGICAL ASSOCIATIONS

STATE	ADDRESS	TELEPHONE NUMBER
New Jersey Psychological Association	349 E. Northfield Road, Suite 211, Livingston, NJ 07039-4806	201-535-9888
New Mexico Psychological Association	2501 San Pedro N.E., Suite 113, Albuquerque, NM 87110	505-883-7376
New York State Psychological Association	Executive Park East, Albany, NY 12203	518-437-1040
North Carolina Psychological Association	1004 Dresser Court, Suite 106, Raleigh, NC 27609-7353	919-872-1005
North Dakota Psychological Association	116 N. 4th St., Suite 130, Bismarck, ND 58501-2486	701-223-9045
Ohio Psychological Association	400 East Town Street, Suite 020, Columbus, OH 43215-1599	614-224-0034
Oklahoma Psychological Association	P.O. Box 18508, 708 N.E. 42nd Street, Oklahoma City, OK 73154-0508	405-424-0019
Oregon Psychological Association	147 N.E. 102nd, Portland, OR 97216	503-253-9155
Pennsylvania Psychological Association	416 Forster Street, Harrisburg, PA 17102-1714	717-232-3817
Rhode Island Psychological Association	Independence Square, 500 Prospect Street, Pawtucket, RI 02860-6260	401-728-5570
South Carolina Psychological Association	P.O. Box 5207, Columbia, SC 29250-5207	803-771-6050
South Dakota Psychological Association	1208 Elkhorn St., Sioux Falls, SD 57104	605-332-3386
Tennessee Psychological Association	530 Church Street, Suite 300, Nashville, TN 37219-2394	615-254-3687
Texas Psychological Association	6633 E. Highway 290, Suite 305, Austin, TX 78723-1158	512-454-2449
Utah Psychological Association	2102 East 3780 South, Salt Lake City, UT 84109	801-278-4665
Virginia Psychological Association	109 Amherst Street, Winchester, VA 22601-4182	703-667-5544

STATE	ADDRESS	TELEPHONE NUMBER
Vermont Psychological Association	P.O. Box 1017, Montpelier, VT 05601-1017	802-229-5447
Washington State Psychological Association	P.O. Box 2016, Edmonds, WA 98020-2016	206-363-9772
West Virginia Psychological Association	P.O. Box 536, Scott Depot, WV 25560	304-757-0458
Wisconsin Psychological Association	121 South Hancock Street, Madison, WI 53703-3461	608-251-1450
Wyoming Psychological Association	P.O. Box 1191, Laramie, WY 82070-1191	307-745-3167

APPENDIX 2:

RESOURCE DIRECTORY FOR VICTIMS—GENERAL

NAME	ADDRESS	TELEPHONE NUMBER
American Association for Counseling	5999 Stevenson Avenue, Alexandria, VA 22304	703-823-9800
American Bar Association, Victims Committee	1800 M Street N.W., 2nd Floor South, Washington, DC 20036	202-331-2260
American Civil Liberties Union	132 West 43rd Street, New York, NY 10036	212-944-9800
Citizen Action	1300 Connecticut Avenue N.W., Suite 401, Washington, DC 20036	202-857-5153
The Compassionate Friends	P.O. Box 1347, Oak Brook, IL 60521	312-990-0010
Concerns of Police Survivors	P.O. Box 3199, Camdenton, MO 65020	800-784-2677
Family and Friends of Missing Persons and Violent Crime Victims	P.O. Box 27529, Seattle, WA 98125	206-362-1081
Handgun Control	1225 I Street N.W., Washington, DC 20005	202-898-0792
Institute for Victims of Trauma	6801 Market Square Drive, McLean, VA 22101	703-847-8456
National Association of Crime Victim Compensation Boards	P.O. Box 16003, Alexandria, VA 22302	703-370-2996
The National Center for Citizen Involvement	1111 Nineteenth Street North, Arlington, VA 20005	703-276-0542
National Crime Prevention Council	1700 K Street N.W., 2nd Floor, Washington, DC 20006	202-466-6272
National Criminal Justice Association	444 North Capitol Street N.W., Washington, DC 20001	202-347-4900

NAME	ADDRESS	TELEPHONE NUMBER
National Organization for Victim Assistance (NOVA)	1757 Park Road N.W., Washington, DC 20010	202-232-6682
National Victim Center	307 West Seventh Street, Suite 1001, Fort Worth, TX 76102	817-877-3855
No Greater Love	1750 New York Avenue N.W., Washington, DC 20006	202-783-4665
Office for Victims of Crime, U.S. Department of Justice	633 Indiana Avenue N.W., 13th Floor, Washington, DC 20531	202-724-5947
The Society for Traumatic Stress Studies	P.O. Box 1564, Lancaster, PA 17603	717 396-8877
They Help Each Other Spiritually National Headquarters	410 Penn Hills Mall, Pittsburgh, PA 15235	412-471-7779
Trial Lawyers for Public Justice	1625 Massachusetts Avenue N.W., Suite 100, Washington, DC 20036	202-797-8600
U.S. Association for Victim/Offender Mediation	254 South Morgan Boulevard, Valparaiso, IN 46383	219-462-1127

APPENDIX 3:

CRIMINAL JUSTICE RESOURCES

NAME	ADDRESS	TELEPHONE NUMBER
American Bar Association, Section on Criminal Justice	1800 M Street N.W., Washington, DC 20036	202-331-2260
American Civil Liberties Union	132 West 43rd Street, New York, NY 10036	212-944-9800
American Correctional Association	8025 Laurel Lakes Court, Laurel, MD 20707-5075	800-ACA-JOIN
American Jail Association	2053 Day Road, Suite 100, Hagerstown, MD 21740-9795	301-790-3930
American Probation and Parole Association	P.O. Box 11910, Lexington, KY 40578-1910	606-244-8000
The Association of Trial Lawyers of America	1050 Thirty-First Street N.W., Washington, DC 20007	202-965-3500
Center for Civil Rights	216 G Street N.E., Washington, DC 20002	202-546-6045
Center for Constitutional Rights (CCR)	666 Broadway, New York, NY 10012	212-614-6464
Executive Office for U.S. Attorneys, U.S. Department of Justice	Patrick Henry Building, Room 6010, 601 D Street N.W., Washington, DC 20530	202-616-6792
Federal Bureau of Investigation, Victim-Witness Assistance Program	J. Edgar Hoover FBI Building, Room 3150, Washington, DC 20535	202-324-5968
Federal Bureau of Prisons, Victim-Witness Assistance Program	U.S. Department of Justice, 320 First Street N.W., Room 536, Washington, DC 20534	800-359-3267
International Association of Chiefs of Police	515 North Washington Street, Alexandria, VA 22314	800-THE-IACP
National Association of Attorneys General	Hall of States, 444 North Capitol Street N.W., Suite 339, Washington, DC 20001	202-434-8000

NAME	ADDRESS	TELEPHONE NUMBER
National Criminal Justice Association	444 North Capitol Street N.W., Washington, DC 20001	202-347-4900
National District Attorney's Association	99 Canal Center Plaza, Suite 510, Alexandria, VA 22314	703-549-4401
National Institute for Citizen Education in the Law	24 E. Street N.W., Suite 400, Washington, DC 20001	202-662-9620
National Organization of Black Law Enforcement Executives	908 Pennsylvania Avenue S.E., Washington, DC 20003-2227	202-546-8811
National Prison Project	161 P Street N.W., Suite 340, Washington, DC 20036	202-331-0500
National Sheriff's Association	1450 Duke Street, Alexandria, VA 22314-3490	800-424-7827
National Victims Resource Center	P.O. Box 6000, Rockville, MD 20850	800-627-6872
The Sentencing Project	918 F Street N.W., Suite 501, Washington, DC 20004	202-628-0871
Trial Lawyers for Public Justice	1625 Massachusetts Avenue N.W., Suite 100, Washington, DC 20036	202-797-8600

APPENDIX 4:

STATE VICTIM COMPENSATION PROGRAMS

STATE	ADDRESS	TELEPHONE NUMBER
Alabama Crime Victims Compensation Commission	P.O. Box 1548, Montgomery, AL 3610	205-242-4007
Alaska Violent Crime Compensation Board	P.O. Box 111200, Juneau, AK 99811	907-465-3040
Arizona Criminal Justice Commission	1501 West Washington, Suite 207, Phoenix, AZ 85007	602-542-1928
Arkansas Crime Victims Reparations Board	601 Tower Building, 323 Center Street, Little Rock, AR 72201	501-682-1323
California Victims of Crime Program	P.O. Box 3036, Sacramento, CA 95812	916-323-6251
Colorado Division of Criminal Justice	700 Kipling Street, Suite 3000, Denver, CO 80215	303-271-6840
Connecticut Commission on Victim Services	1155 Silas Deane Highway, Wethersfield, CT 06109	203-529-3089
Delaware Violent Crime Compensation Board	1500 East Newport Pike, Suite 10, Wilmington, DE 19804	302-995-8383
District of Columbia Crime Victims Compensation Program	1200 Upshur Street N.W., Washington, DC 20011	202-576-7706
Florida Division of Victim Services	The Capitol PL-01, Tallahassee, FL 32399	904-488-0848
Georgia Crime Victim Compensation Program	503 Oak Place South, Suite 540, Atlanta, GA 30349	404-559-4949
Hawaii Criminal Injuries Compensation Commission	335 Merchant Street, Suite 244, Honolulu, HI 96813	808-587-1143
Idaho Victim Compensation Program	317 Main Street, Boise, ID 83720	208-334-6000
Illinois Crime Victims Division	100 W. Randolf, 13th Floor, Chicago, IL 60601	312-814-2581

VICTIM'S RIGHTS LAW

STATE	ADDRESS	TELEPHONE NUMBER
Indiana Violent Crimes Victim Compensation Division	402 W. Washington Street, Room W-382, Indianapolis, IN 46204	317-232-3809
Iowa Crime Victim Assistance Program	Old Historical Building, Des Moines, IA 50319	515-281-5044
Kansas Crime Victims Reparations Board	700 S.W. Jackson, Suite 400, Topeka, KS 66603	913-296-2359
Kentucky Crime Victims Compensation Board	115 Myrtle Avenue, Frankfort, KY 40601	502-564-2290
Louisiana Crime Victims Reparations Board	1885 Wooddale Boulevard, Suite 708, Baton Rouge, LA 70806	504-925-4437
Maine Crime Victim Compensation Program	State House Station #6, Augusta, ME 04333	207-626-8589
Maryland Criminal Injuries Compensation Board	6776 Reisterstown Road, Suite 313, Baltimore, MD 21215	410-764-4214
Massachusetts Victims Compensation and Assistance	One Ashburton Place, Boston, MA 02108	617-727-2300
Michigan Crime Victims Compensation Board	P.O. Box 30026, Lansing, MI 48909	517-373-7373
Minnesota Crime Victims Reparations Board	1821 University Avenue, Suite N465, St. Paul, MN 55104	612-642-0395
Mississippi Crime Victim Compensation Program	P.O. Box 267, Jackson, MS 39205	800-829-6766
Missouri Crime Victims Compensation Unit	P.O. Box 58, Jefferson City, MO 65102	314-525-6006
Montana Crime Victims Unit	303 North Roberts, 4th Floor, Helena, MT 59620	406-444-3653
Nebraska Commission on Law Enforcement	P.O. Box 94946, Lincoln, NE 68509	402-471-2828
Nevada Victims of Crime Program	2770 Maryland Parkway, Suite 416, Las Vegas, NV 89109	702-486-7259

STATE VICTIM COMPENSATION PROGRAMS

STATE	ADDRESS	TELEPHONE NUMBER
New Hampshire Victims Compensation Program	State House Annex, Concord, NH 03301	603-271-1284
New Jersey Violent Crimes Compensation Board	60 Park Place, Suite 10, Newark, NJ 07102	201-648-2107
New Mexico Crime Victims Reparations Commission	8100 Mountain Road N.E., Suite 106, Albuquerque, NM 87110	505-841-9432
New York Crime Victims Board	270 Broadway, Room 200, New York, NY 10007	212-417-5133
North Carolina Victim and Justice Services	P.O. Box 27687, Raleigh, NC 27611	919-733-7974
North Dakota Crime Victims Reparations Program	P.O. Box 5521, Bismarck, ND 58502	701-221-6195
Ohio Victims of Crime Compensation Program	65 East State Street, Suite 1100, Columbus, OH 43215	614-466-7190
Oklahoma Crime Victims Compensation Board	2200 Classen Boulevard, Suite 1800., Oklahoma City, OK 73106	405-557-6704
Oregon Crime Victims Assistance Section	Department of Justice, 100 Justice Building, Salem, OR 97310	503-378-5348
Pennsylvania Crime Victims Compensation Board	333 Market Street, Lobby Level, Harrisburg, PA 17191	717-783-5153
Rhode Island Judicial Planning Section, Supreme Court	250 Benefit Street, Providence, RI 02903	401-227-2500
South Carolina Division of Victim Assistance	P.O. Box 210009, Columbia, SC 29221	803-737-8142
South Dakota Crime Victims Compensation Commission	115 East Dakota Avenue, Pierre, SD 57501	605-773-3478
Tennessee Division of Claims Administration	Andrew Jackson Building, 11th Floor, Volunteer Plaza, Nashville, TN 37243	615-741-2734
Texas Crime Victim Compensations Division	P.O. Box 12548, Capitol Station, Austin, TX 78711	512-462-6400

STATE	ADDRESS	TELEPHONE NUMBER
Utah Office of Crime Victim Reparations	350 East 500 South, Suite 200, Salt Lake City, UT 84111	801-533-4000
Vermont Center for Crime Victim Services	P.O. Box 991, Montpelier, VT 05601	802-828-3374
Virginia Crime Victims Compensation Division	P.O. Box 5423, Richmond, VA 23220	804-367-8686
Washington Crime Victim Compensation Program	P.O. Box 44520, Olympia, WA 98504	206-956-5340
West Virginia Crime Victim Compensation	1900 Kanawha Boulevard East, Building 1, Room 6, Charleston, WV 25305	304-558-3471
Wisconsin Office of Crime Victim Services	P.O. Box 7951, Madison, WI 53707	608-266-6470
Wyoming Crime Victims Compensation Commission	1700 Westland Road, Cheyenne, WY 82002	307-635-4050

APPENDIX 5:

ELIGIBLE PERSONS UNDER STATE VICTIM COMPENSATION STATUTES[1]

STATE	ELIGIBLE PERSONS
Alabama	Injured party, spouse, children, parents and siblings
Alaska	Injured party, spouse, children, parents and siblings
Arizona	Injured party, spouse, children, parents and siblings
Arkansas	Injured party, spouse, children, parents and siblings
California	Injured party, spouse, children, parents and siblings
Colorado	Families and secondary victims
Connecticut	Injured party, spouse, children, parents and siblings
Delaware	Injured party, spouse, children, parents and siblings
District of Columbia	Injured party, spouse, children, and parents of victim when victim is killed
Florida	Injured party, spouse, children, parents and siblings
Georgia	Injured party, spouse, children, parents, guardian and "Good Samaritans"
Hawaii	Injured party, spouse, children, parents and siblings
Idaho	Injured party, spouse, children, parents and siblings
Illinois	Injured party
Indiana	Injured party, spouse, children, parents and siblings
Iowa	Injured party, spouse, children, parents and siblings
Kansas	Injured party, spouse, children and parents
Kentucky	Injured party, spouse, children, parents and siblings
Louisiana	Injured party, spouse, children and parents

---

[1] Ginsburg, William L., Victims' Rights: The Complete Guide to Crime Victim Compensation, Sphinx Publishing, 1994

STATE	ELIGIBLE PERSONS
Maine	Injured party
Maryland	Injured party, spouse, children, parents and siblings
Massachusetts	Injured party, spouse, children, parents and siblings
Michigan	Injured party, spouse, children, parents and siblings
Minnesota	Injured party, spouse, children, parents and siblings
Mississippi	Injured party, spouse and children
Missouri	Injured party, spouse, children, parents and siblings
Montana	Injured party, spouse, children, parents and siblings
Nebraska	Injured party, spouse, children, parents and siblings
Nevada	Injured party, spouse, children and parents
New Hampshire	Injured party, spouse, children and parents
New Jersey	Injured party, spouse, children, parents and siblings
New Mexico	Injured party, spouse, children, parents and siblings
New York	Injured party, spouse, children, parents and siblings
North Carolina	Injured party, spouse, children, parents and siblings
North Dakota	Injured party
Ohio	Injured party, dependent of deceased victim, someone who has paid the expenses of the victim and "Good Samaritans"
Oklahoma	Injured party, spouse, children, parents and siblings
Oregon	Injured party, spouse, children, parents and siblings
Pennsylvania	Injured party, spouse, children, parents and siblings
Rhode Island	Injured party, spouse, children, parents and siblings
South Carolina	Injured party, spouse, children, parents and siblings
South Dakota	Injured party, spouse, children, parents and "Good Samaritans"
Tennessee	Injured party, spouse, children, parents and siblings
Texas	Injured party, spouse, children, parents and siblings

STATE VICTIM COMPENSATION—ELIGIBLE PERSONS

STATE	ELIGIBLE PERSONS
Utah	Injured party, spouse, children, parents and siblings
Vermont	Injured party and dependents
Virginia	Injured party, spouse, children, parents and siblings
Washington	Injured party, spouse, children, parents and siblings
West Virginia	Injured party, spouse, children, parents and siblings
Wisconsin	Injured party, spouse, children, parents and siblings
Wyoming	Injured party, spouse, children, parents and siblings

APPENDIX 6:

COMPENSABLE CRIMES UNDER STATE VICTIM COMPENSATION STATUTES[1]

STATE	ELIGIBLE PERSONS
Alabama	Assault and battery, child physical and/or sexual abuse, domestic abuse, drunk driving, homicide, motor vehicle crime, rape, robbery, sex offenses and spousal abuse
Alaska	Assault and battery, child physical and/or sexual abuse, domestic abuse, drunk driving, homicide, motor vehicle crime, rape, robbery, sex offenses and spousal abuse
Arizona	Assault and battery, child physical and/or sexual abuse, domestic abuse, drunk driving, homicide, rape, robbery, sex offenses and spousal abuse
Arkansas	Assault and battery, child physical and/or sexual abuse, domestic abuse, drunk driving, homicide, motor vehicle crime, rape, robbery, sex offenses and spousal abuse
California	Assault and battery, child physical and/or sexual abuse, domestic abuse, drunk driving, homicide, motor vehicle crime, rape, robbery, sex offenses and spousal abuse
Colorado	Assault and battery, child physical and/or sexual abuse, domestic abuse, drunk driving, homicide, motor vehicle crime, rape, robbery, sex offenses and spousal abuse
Connecticut	Assault and battery, child physical and/or sexual abuse, domestic abuse, drunk driving, homicide, motor vehicle crime, rape, robbery, sex offenses and spousal abuse
Delaware	Assault and battery, child physical and/or sexual abuse, domestic abuse, drunk driving, homicide, motor vehicle crime, rape, robbery, sex offenses and spousal abuse
District of Columbia	Assault and battery, child physical and/or sexual abuse, domestic abuse, drunk driving, homicide, motor vehicle crime, rape, robbery, sex offenses and spousal abuse
Florida	Assault and battery, child physical and/or sexual abuse, drunk driving, homicide, rape, robbery, sex offenses

---

[1] Ginsburg, William L., Victims' Rights: The Complete Guide to Crime Victim Compensation, Sphinx Publishing, 1994

STATE	ELIGIBLE PERSONS
Georgia	Assault and battery, child physical and/or sexual abuse, domestic abuse, homicide, motor vehicle crime
Hawaii	Assault and battery, child physical and/or sexual abuse, domestic abuse, homicide, motor vehicle crime, rape, robbery and sex offenses
Idaho	Assault and battery, child physical and/or sexual abuse, domestic abuse, drunk driving, homicide, motor vehicle crime, rape, robbery, sex offenses and spousal abuse
Illinois	Assault and battery, child physical and/or sexual abuse, domestic abuse, drunk driving, homicide, rape, sex offenses and spousal abuse
Indiana	Assault and battery, child physical and/or sexual abuse, domestic abuse, drunk driving, homicide, motor vehicle crime, rape, robbery, sex offenses and spousal abuse
Iowa	Assault and battery, child physical and/or sexual abuse, domestic abuse, drunk driving, homicide, motor vehicle crime, rape, robbery, sex offenses and spousal abuse
Kansas	Assault and battery, child physical and/or sexual abuse, domestic abuse, drunk driving, homicide, rape, sex offenses and spousal abuse
Kentucky	Assault and battery, child physical and/or sexual abuse, drunk driving, homicide, rape and sex offenses
Louisiana	Assault and battery, child physical and/or sexual abuse, domestic abuse, homicide, motor vehicle crime, rape, robbery, sex offenses and spousal abuse
Maine	Assault and battery, child physical and/or sexual abuse, domestic abuse, drunk driving, homicide, motor vehicle crime, robbery and sex offenses
Maryland	Assault and battery, child physical and/or sexual abuse, domestic abuse, drunk driving, homicide, motor vehicle crime, rape, sex offenses and spousal abuse
Massachusetts	Assault and battery, child physical and/or sexual abuse, domestic abuse, drunk driving, homicide, motor vehicle crime, rape, robbery, sex offenses and spousal abuse
Michigan	Assault and battery, child physical and/or sexual abuse, domestic abuse, drunk driving, homicide, motor vehicle crime, rape, robbery, sex offenses and spousal abuse
Minnesota	Assault and battery, child physical and/or sexual abuse, domestic abuse, drunk driving, homicide, rape, robbery, sex offenses and spousal abuse

STATE VICTIM COMPENSATION—COMPENSABLE CRIMES

STATE	ELIGIBLE PERSONS
Mississippi	Assault and battery, child physical and/or sexual abuse, domestic abuse, drunk driving, homicide, motor vehicle crime, rape, robbery, sex offenses and spousal abuse
Missouri	Assault and battery, child physical and/or sexual abuse, domestic abuse, drunk driving, homicide, motor vehicle crime, rape, sex offenses and spousal abuse
Montana	Assault and battery, child physical and/or sexual abuse, domestic abuse, homicide, rape, robbery, sex offenses and spousal abuse
Nebraska	Assault and battery, child physical and/or sexual abuse, domestic abuse, drunk driving, homicide, rape, sex offenses and spousal abuse
Nevada	Assault and battery, child physical and/or sexual abuse, domestic abuse, drunk driving, homicide, rape, robbery, sex offenses and spousal abuse
New Hampshire	Assault and battery, child physical and/or sexual abuse, domestic abuse, drunk driving, homicide, motor vehicle crime, rape, robbery, sex offenses and spousal abuse
New Jersey	Assault and battery, child physical and/or sexual abuse, domestic abuse, homicide, rape, robbery, sex offenses and spousal abuse
New Mexico	Assault and battery, child sexual abuse, drunk driving, homicide, motor vehicle crime and rape
New York	Assault and battery, child physical and/or sexual abuse, domestic abuse, drunk driving, homicide, motor vehicle crime, rape, robbery, sex offenses and spousal abuse
North Carolina	Assault and battery, child physical and/or sexual abuse, domestic abuse, homicide, motor vehicle crime, rape, robbery, sex offenses and spousal abuse
North Dakota	Assault and battery, child physical and/or sexual abuse, domestic abuse, drunk driving, homicide, rape, robbery, sex offenses and spousal abuse
Ohio	Assault and battery, child physical and/or sexual abuse, domestic abuse, homicide, motor vehicle crime, rape, robbery, sex offenses and spousal abuse
Oklahoma	Assault and battery, child physical and/or sexual abuse, domestic abuse, homicide, motor vehicle crime, rape, robbery, sex offenses and spousal abuse

STATE	ELIGIBLE PERSONS
Oregon	Assault and battery, child physical and/or sexual abuse, domestic abuse, drunk driving, homicide, motor vehicle crime, rape, robbery, sex offenses and spousal abuse
Pennsylvania	Assault and battery, child physical and/or sexual abuse, domestic abuse, homicide, rape, robbery, sex offenses and spousal abuse
Rhode Island	Assault and battery, child physical and/or sexual abuse, domestic abuse, drunk driving, homicide, motor vehicle crime, rape, robbery, sex offenses and spousal abuse
South Carolina	Assault and battery, child physical and/or sexual abuse, domestic abuse, drunk driving, homicide, motor vehicle crime, rape and sex offenses
South Dakota	Assault and battery, child physical and/or sexual abuse, domestic abuse, drunk driving, homicide, motor vehicle crime, rape, robbery, sex offenses and spousal abuse
Tennessee	Assault and battery, child physical and/or sexual abuse, domestic abuse, drunk driving, homicide, rape, robbery, sex offenses and spousal abuse
Texas	Assault and battery, child physical and/or sexual abuse, domestic abuse, drunk driving, homicide, motor vehicle crime, rape, robbery, sex offenses and spousal abuse
Utah	Assault and battery, child physical and/or sexual abuse, domestic abuse, drunk driving, homicide, motor vehicle crime, rape, robbery, sex offenses and spousal abuse
Vermont	Assault and battery, child sexual abuse, domestic abuse, drunk driving, homicide and sex offenses
Virginia	Assault and battery, child physical and/or sexual abuse, domestic abuse, drunk driving, homicide, rape, robbery, sex offenses and spousal abuse
Washington	Assault and battery, child physical and/or sexual abuse, domestic abuse, drunk driving, homicide, motor vehicle crime, rape, robbery, sex offenses and spousal abuse
West Virginia	Assault and battery, child physical and/or sexual abuse, domestic abuse, drunk driving, homicide, motor vehicle crime, rape, robbery, sex offenses and spousal abuse
Wisconsin	Assault and battery, child physical and/or sexual abuse, domestic abuse, drunk driving, homicide, motor vehicle crime, rape, robbery, sex offenses and spousal abuse

STATE	ELIGIBLE PERSONS
Wyoming	Assault and battery, child physical and/or sexual abuse, domestic abuse, drunk driving, homicide, rape, robbery, sex offenses and spousal abuse

APPENDIX 7:

MAXIMUM COMPENSATION AVAILABLE UNDER STATE VICTIM COMPENSATION STATUTES[1]

STATE	MAXIMUM AWARD OF COMPENSATION
Alabama	$10,000
Alaska	$40,000
Arizona	$10,000
Arkansas	$10,000
California	$6,000
Colorado	$10,000
Connecticut	$25,000
Delaware	$25,000
District of Columbia	$25,000
Florida	$10,000
Georgia	$1,000
Hawaii	$10,000
Idaho	$25,000
Illinois	$25,000
Indiana	$10,000
Iowa	$20,600
Kansas	$10,000
Kentucky	$25,000
Louisiana	$10,000

---

[1] Ginsburg, William L., Victims' Rights: The Complete Guide to Crime Victim Compensation, Sphinx Publishing, 1994

STATE	MAXIMUM AWARD OF COMPENSATION
Maine	$5,000
Maryland	$45,000
Massachusetts	$25,000
Michigan	$25,000
Minnesota	$50,000
Mississippi	$10,000
Missouri	$10,000
Montana	$25,000
Nebraska	$10,000
Nevada	$15,000
New Hampshire	$5,000
New Jersey	$25,000
New Mexico	$12,500
New York	unlimited
North Carolina	$22,000
North Dakota	$25,000
Ohio	$50,000
Oklahoma	$10,000
Oregon	$23,000
Pennsylvania	$35,000
Rhode Island	$25,000
South Carolina	$10,000
South Dakota	$10,000
Tennessee	$5,000
Texas	$25,000

STATE VICTIM MAXIMUM COMPENSATION

STATE	MAXIMUM AWARD OF COMPENSATION
Utah	$50,000
Vermont	$10,000
Virginia	$15,000
Washington	$20,000
West Virginia	$50,000
Wisconsin	$40,000
Wyoming	$10,000

APPENDIX 8:

THE VICTIMS JUSTICE ACT OF 1995

TITLE I: RESTITUTION

Amends the Federal criminal code to require the court to order restitution of the victim when a convicted defendant is being sentenced for specified offenses (see Sec. 103).

Authorizes the court to order restitution in certain other cases.

Makes specified procedures (see Sec.105) applicable to all orders of restitution.

Requires the court to provide, as an explicit condition of a sentence of probation, that the defendant make restitution as ordered, pay the assessment imposed, and notify the court of any material change in his or her economic circumstances that might affect his or her ability to pay restitution, fines, or special assessments.

Repeals specified restrictions on the court's authority to order the making of restitution.

SECTION 103

Directs the court to order, in addition to any other penalty authorized by law, that the defendant make restitution to the victim of the offense or, if the victim is deceased, to the victim's estate.

Defines "victim" as a person directly and proximately harmed as a result of the commission of an offense for which restitution may be ordered, including any person directly harmed by the defendant's criminal conduct in the course of an offense that involves a scheme, conspiracy, or pattern of criminal activity.

Permits a legal guardian or the representative of the victim's estate (other than the defendant), another family member, or any other person appointed as suitable by the court to assume the victim's rights in the case of a victim who is under age 18, incompetent, incapacitated, or deceased.

Sets forth provisions regarding:

(1) restitution to persons other than the victim;

(2) the form and amount of restitution; and

(3) plea agreements not resulting in a conviction.

Requires restitution in all sentencing proceedings for convictions of, or plea agreements relating to charges for, any offense:

(1) that is a crime of violence, an offense against property (including fraud), or an offense relating to tampering with consumer products; or

(2) in which an identifiable victim has suffered a physical injury or pecuniary loss.

Makes exceptions where the number of identifiable victims is so large as to make restitution impracticable or where determining complex issues of fact or the amount of the victim's losses would create an excessive burden on the sentencing process.

SECTION 104

Authorizes the court, when sentencing a defendant convicted of specified offenses under the Controlled Substances Act (CSA), to order that the defendant make restitution to any victim of such offense.

Specifies that a participant in an offense may not be considered a victim of the offense.

Specifies that, in determining whether to order restitution, the court:

(1) shall consider the amount of the loss sustained by each victim as a result of the offense, the financial resources of the defendant, the financial needs and earning ability of the defendant and the defendant's dependents, and such other factors as the court deems appropriate; and

(2) may decline to order restitution upon determining that the complication and prolongation of the sentencing process resulting from fashioning such an order outweighs the need to provide restitution to any victims.

Sets forth provisions regarding situations in which there is no identifiable victim.

Directs that an order of restitution in such case be based on the amount of public harm caused by the offense.

Limits the amount of such restitution ordered to the amount of the fine ordered for the offense charged in the case.

Directs that such restitution be distributed as follows: 65 percent to the Victim Assistance Administration of the State in which the crime occurred and 35 percent to the State entity designated to receive Federal substance abuse block grant funds.

Prohibits the court from making an award if it appears likely that such award would interfere with a civil or criminal forfeiture.

Specifies that certain penalty assessments or fines shall take precedence over a restitution order.

Directs that requests for community restitution be considered in all plea agreements negotiated by the United States.

Requires the Commission to promulgate guidelines to assist courts in determining the amount of restitution that may be ordered.

Prohibits any restitution from being ordered under this section until such time as the Commission promulgates its guidelines.

Makes conforming changes to the Violence Against Women Act of 1994 and to telemarketing fraud provisions of the Federal criminal code.

SECTION 105

Revises procedures for the issuance and enforcement of restitution orders.

Directs the court to:

(1) order the probation service of the court to obtain and include in its presentence report, or in a separate report, information sufficient for the court to exercise its discretion in fashioning a restitution order (which shall include a complete accounting of the losses to each victim, any restitution owed pursuant to a plea agreement, and information relating to the economic circumstances of each defendant); and

(2) disclose to both the defendant and the attorney for the Government all portions of the report pertaining to such matters. Directs the probation service to inform the court if the number or identity of victims cannot be reasonably ascertained, or other circumstances exist that make such requirement impracticable.

Makes specified provisions of the Federal criminal code and Rule 32(c) of the Federal Rules of Criminal Procedure the only rules applicable to proceedings for the issuance and enforcement of restitution orders.

Directs the attorney for the Government, within 60 days after conviction and not later than ten days prior to sentencing, to:

(1) provide the probation service of the court with a listing of the amounts subject to restitution, after consulting with all identified victims;

(2) provide notice to all such victims of the offenses of which the defendant was convicted, the listing of amounts subject to restitution, the victim's right to submit information concerning losses, and the scheduled date, time, and place of the sentencing hearing;

(3) advise any victim that he or she may file a separate affidavit relating to his or her losses.

Directs each defendant (within such time frame) to prepare and file with the probation service an affidavit fully describing the defendant's financial resources.

Authorizes the court, after reviewing the report of the probation service, to require additional documentation or hear testimony.

Specifies that the privacy of any such records filed or testimony heard shall be maintained and such records may be filed or testimony heard in camera.

Directs the attorney for the Government to inform the court if the victim's losses are not ascertainable ten days prior to sentencing and the court shall set a date for the final determination of the victim's losses.

Provides a victim who subsequently discovers further losses 60 days after discovery to petition the court for an amended restitution order (which order may be granted only upon a showing of good cause for the failure to include such losses in the initial claim for restitutionary relief).

Sets forth provisions regarding referral of any issue arising in connection with a proposed restitution order to a magistrate or special master.

Directs the court to order restitution to each victim in the full amount of each victim's losses as determined by the court without consideration of the defendant's economic circumstances.

Sets forth further requirements, including provisions regarding the form of payments, situations involving multiple defendants, a prohibition on considering the fact that a victim has received compensation with respect to a loss from insurance or any other source in determining the amount of restitution, notification of material changes in the defendant's circumstances, of the payment schedule as the interests of justice require.

Specifies that:

(1) a defendant's conviction for an offense involving the act giving rise to a restitution order shall estop the defendant from denying the essential allegations of that offense in any subsequent Federal civil pro-

ceeding or State civil proceeding, to the extent consistent with State law, brought by the victim; and

(2) a restitution order may be enforced by the United States, as specified, or by a victim named in the order, in the same manner as a judgment in a civil action.

Requires a person obligated to provide restitution or pay a fine who receives substantial resources from any source, including inheritance, settlement, or other judgment, during a period of incarceration, to apply the value of such resources to any restitution or fine still owed.

SECTION 106

Amends Rule 32(b) of the Federal Rules of Criminal Procedure to require that:

(1) a presentence investigation and report, or other report containing information sufficient for the court to enter an order of restitution, be required in any case in which restitution is required to be ordered; and

(2) a presentence report contain, in appropriate cases, information sufficient for the court to enter an order of restitution.

Adds restitution to existing provisions governing the imposition of a fine in Federal criminal cases. Directs the court to impose a fine or other monetary penalty only to the extent that such fine or penalty will not impair the ability of the defendant to make restitution required to a victim other than the United States.

Sets forth provisions regarding payment schedules, notification to the court of material changes in the defendant's economic circumstances, and default on a restitution fine or payment.

Adds restitution provisions to provisions governing the post-sentence administration of fines, including collection.

Makes it the responsibility of each victim to notify the Attorney General or the appropriate court entity of any change in the victim's mailing address while restitution is still owed.

Directs that the confidentiality of any information relating to a victim be maintained.

Sets priorities for the disbursement of money received from a defendant.

Authorizes the court, upon a finding that the defendant is in default on a payment of a fine or restitution, to revoke or modify the terms or conditions of probation or a term of supervised release, resentence a defendant, hold the defendant in contempt of court, enter a restraining order or injunction, order the sale of property of the defendant, accept a performance bond, enter or adjust a payment schedule, or take any other action necessary to obtain compliance with the order of a fine or restitution.

Allows any hearing arising out of such default to be conducted by a magistrate judge, subject to de novo review by the court.

Requires that proceedings in which the participation of a defendant who is confined in a correctional facility is required or permitted be conducted by telephone, video conference, or other communications technology without removing the prisoner from the facility.

Prohibits incarcerating a defendant solely on the basis of inability to make payments because of indigency.

SECTION 107

Directs the United States Sentencing Commission to amend or promulgate guidelines to reflect this Act and the amendments made by this Act.

SECTION 108

Requires the Attorney General to amend or promulgate guidelines to carry out this Act and to ensure that:

>(1) in all plea agreements negotiated by the United States, consideration is given to requesting that the defendant provide full restitution to all the victims; and

>(2) restitution orders are enforced to the fullest extent of the law.

SECTION 109

Doubles the special assessments on persons convicted of a felony in Federal cases.

TITLE II: MISCELLANEOUS PROVISIONS

Amends the Victims of Crime Act of 1984 to:

>(1) prohibit payments to delinquent criminal debtors by State crime victim compensation programs; and

>(2) exclude victim assistance from income for purposes of determining eligibility for Federal benefits.

SECTION 202

Authorizes the Director of the Office for Victims of Crime to make supplemental grants to States:

(1) to provide compensation and assistance to residents who, while outside the United States, are victims of a terrorist act or mass violence, subject to specified limitations; and

(2) for eligible crime victim compensation and assistance programs to provide emergency relief for the benefit of victims of domestic terrorist acts or mass violence and to provide funding to U.S. Attorney's Offices for use in coordination with State efforts in providing emergency relief.

Sets forth or revises provisions regarding the funding of compensation and assistance to victims of terrorism, mass violence, and crime, the use of unobligated funds, and the base amount.

SECTION 203

Sets forth provisions regarding the severability of this Act.

SECTION 204

Directs:

(1) the Attorney General, in cooperation with the Director of the Administrative Office of the United States Courts, to conduct a study of the funds paid out of the Crime Victims Fund and the impact that the amendments made by this Act have on sums available in the Fund; and

(2) the Attorney General and the Director to report interim findings to the Chairman and ranking Member of the House and Senate Judiciary Committees.

APPENDIX 9:

RESOURCE DIRECTORY FOR VICTIMS—WOMEN

NAME	ADDRESS	TELEPHONE NUMBER
ACTION	1100 Vermont Avenue N.W., Washington, DC 20525	202-934-9396
Black, Indian, Hispanic and Asian Women in Action	122 West Franklin Avenue, Suite 306, Minneapolis, MN 55404	612-870-1193
Center for the Prevention of Sexual and Domestic Violence	1914 North 34th Street, Suite 105, Seattle, WA 98103	800-562-6025
Center for Women Policy Studies	2000 P Street N.W., Suite 508, Washington, DC 20036	202-872-1770
EMERGE	280 Green Street, 2nd Floor, Cambridge, MA 02139	617-547-9870
National Center for Women and Family Law	799 Broadway, Room 402, New York, NY 10003	212-674-8200
National Coalition Against Sexual Assault	2428 Ontario Road N.W., Washington, DC 20009	202-483-7165
National Council on Jewish Women	53 West 23rd Street, New York, NY 10010	212-645-4048
National Organization for Women (NOW)	1000 16th Street N.W., Suite 700, Washington, DC 20036	202-331-0066
Women Against Abuse	P.O. Box 13758, Philadelphia, PA 19101	215-386-1280
Women's Legal Defense Fund	2000 P Street N.W., Suite 400, Washington, DC 20036	202-887-0364

APPENDIX 10:

RESOURCE DIRECTORY FOR VICTIMS—CHILDREN

NAME	ADDRESS	TELEPHONE NUMBER
American Association for Protecting Children	P.O. Box 1266, Denver, CO 80231	800-227-5242
American Bar Association Center on Children and the Law	1800 M Street N.W., Suite 200-S, Washington, DC 20036	202-331-2250
American Professional Society on the Abuse of Children	969 East 60th Street, Chicago, IL 60637	312-702-9419
Children of Murdered Parents	P.O. Box 9317, Whittier, CA 90608	310-699-8427
Council for the Prevention of Child Abuse and Neglect	1305 Fourth Avenue, Room 202, Seattle, WA 98101	206-343-2590
Mothers Against Drunk Driving	511 East John Carpenter Freeway, Suite 700, Irving, TX 75062	800-438-MADD
National Adolescent Sexual Abuse Prevention Project	124D Senatorial Drive, Wilmington, DE 19807	302-654-1102
National Center on Child Abuse and Neglect, U.S. Department of Health and Human Services	P.O. Box 1182, Washington, DC 20013	202-619-0257
Juvenile Justice Clearinghouse	1600 Research Boulevard, Rockville, MD 20850	800-638-8736
National Center for the Prosecution of Child Abuse	1033 North Fairfax Street, Suite 200, Alexandria, VA 22314	703-739-0321
National Child Abuse Coalition	733 Fifteenth Street N.W., Suite 938, Washington, DC 20005	202-247-3666
National Child Abuse Hotline	P.O. Box 630, Hollywood, CA 90028	800-4A-CHILD

NAME	ADDRESS	TELEPHONE NUMBER
National Council on Child Abuse and Family Violence	1155 Connecticut Avenue N.W., Suite 300, Washington, DC 20036	202-429-6695
National Council of Juvenile and Family Court Judges	P.O. Box 8970, Reno, NV 89507	702-784-6012
National Organization of Parents of Murdered Children	100 East Eighth Street, Suite B-41, Cincinnati, OH 45202	513-721-5683
Students Against Driving Drunk	P.O. Box 800, Marlboro, MA 01752	508-481-3568

APPENDIX 11:

RESOURCE DIRECTORY FOR VICTIMS—ELDERLY

NAME	ADDRESS	TELEPHONE NUMBER
American Association of Retired Persons, Division of Criminal Justice	1909 K Street N.W., Washington, DC 20049	202-728-4363
American Bar Association Commission on Legal Problems of the Elderly	1800 M Street N.W., Suite 200, Washington, DC 20036	202-331-2297
Center for Social Gerontology	117 North First Street, Suite 204, Ann Arbor, MI 48104	313-665-1126
Clearinghouse on Abuse and Neglect of the Elderly	University of Delaware, Newark, DE 19716	302-451-2940
The Gerontological Society	1411 K Street N.W., Suite 300, Washington, DC 20005	202-393-1411
Gray Panthers	311 S. Juniper Street, Suite 601, Philadelphia, PA 19107	215-545-6555
Legal Services for the Elderly	132 W. 43rd Street, 3rd Floor, New York, NY 10036	212-595-1340
National Aging Resource Center on Elder Abuse	810 First Street N.E., Suite 500, Washington, DC 20002	202-682-2470
National Association of Area Agencies on Aging	600 Maryland Avenue S.W., Suite 208, Washington, DC 20024	202-484-7520
National Association of State Units on Aging	600 Maryland Avenue S.W., Suite 208, Washington, DC 20024	202-484-7182
National Council of Senior Citizens	925 15th Street, N.W., Washington, DC 20005	203-347-8800
National Council on the Aging	600 Maryland Avenue S.W., West Wing, Suite 100, Washington, DC 20024	202-479-1200
National Indian Council on Aging	P.O. Box 2088, Albuquerque, NM 87103	505-242-9505

National Pacific/Asian Resource Center on Aging	2033 6th Avenue, Suite 410, Seattle, WA 98121	206-448-0313
National Senior Citizens Law Center	1052 W. 6th Street, 7th Floor, Los Angeles, CA 90017	213-482-3550
National Senior Citizens Law Center	2025 M Street N.W., Suite 400, Washington, DC 20036	202-887-5280

APPENDIX 12:

RESOURCE DIRECTORY FOR VICTIMS—HATE CRIMES

NAME	ADDRESS	TELEPHONE NUMBER
American Civil Liberties Union	132 West 43rd Street, New York, NY 10036	212-944-9800
American Indian Law Center	P.O. Box 4456, Station A, Albuquerque, NM 87196	505-277-5462
Anti-Defamation League of the B'nai B'rith	823 United Nations Plaza, New York, NY 10017	212-490-2525
Anti-Violence Project, National Gay and Lesbian Task Force	1517 U Street N.W., Washington, DC 20009	202-332-6483
Black, Indian, Hispanic and Asian Women in Action	122 West Franklin Avenue, Suite 306, Minneapolis, MN 55404	612-870-1193
Center for Civil Rights	216 G Street N.E., Washington, DC 20002	202-546-6045
Center for Constitutional Rights (CCR)	666 Broadway, New York, NY 10012	212-614-6464
Center for Democratic Renewal	P.O. Box 50469, Atlanta, GA 30302	404-221-0025
Cultural Survival, Inc.	53-A Church Street, Cambridge, MA 02138	617-495-2562
NAACP Legal Defense Fund	99 Hudson Street, Suite 160, New York, NY 10013	800-221-7822
National Council of Churches	475 Riverside Drive, New York, NY 10027	212-870-2511
National Council on Jewish Women	53 West 23rd Street, New York, NY 10010	212-645-4048

NAME	ADDRESS	TELEPHONE NUMBER
National Indian Justice Center	The McNear Building, 7 Fourth Street, Suite 28, Petaluma, CA 94952	707-762-8113
National Institute Against Prejudice and Violence	31 South Greene Street, Baltimore, MD 21201	301-328-5170
National Organization of Black Law Enforcement Executives	908 Pennsylvania Avenue S.E., Washington, DC 20003-2227	202-546-8811
National Pacific/Asian Resource Center on Aging	2033 6th Avenue, Suite 410, Seattle, WA 98121	206-448-0313
National Urban League	500 East 62nd Street, New York, NY 10021	800-468-5435
Southern Poverty Law Center	400 Washington Avenue, Montgomery, AL 36104	205-264-2086

GLOSSARY

GLOSSARY

Accusation - An indictment, presentment, information or any other form in which a charge of a crime or offense can be made against an individual.

Accusatory Instrument - The initial pleading which forms the procedural basis for a criminal charge, such as an indictment.

Accuse - To directly and formally institute legal proceedings against a person, charging that he or she has committed an offense.

Acquit - A verdict of "not guilty" which determines that the person is absolved of the charge and prevents a retrial pursuant to the doctrine of double jeopardy.

Acquittal - One who is acquitted receives an acquittal, which is a release without further prosecution.

Adjourn - To briefly postpone or delay a court proceeding.

Adjudication - The determination of a controversy and pronouncement of judgment.

Admissible Evidence - Evidence which may be received by a trial court to assist the trier of fact, either the judge or jury, in deciding a dispute.

Admission - In criminal law, the voluntary acknowledgment that certain facts are true.

American Bar Association (ABA) - A national organization of lawyers and law students.

American Civil Liberties Union (ACLU) - A nationwide organization dedicated to the enforcement and preservation of rights and civil liberties guaranteed by the federal and state constitutions.

Amnesty - A pardon that excuses one of a criminal offense.

Appearance - To come into court, personally or through an attorney, after being summoned.

Arraign - In a criminal proceeding, to accuse one of committing a wrong.

Arraignment - The initial step in the criminal process when the defendant is formally charged with the wrongful conduct.

Arrest - To deprive a person of his liberty by legal authority.

Arson - The crime of intentionally setting fire to a building or other property.

Bail - Security, usually in the form of money, which is given to insure the future attendance of the defendant at all stages of a criminal proceeding.

Bail Bond - A document which secures the release of a person in custody, which is procured by security which is subject to forfeiture if the individual fails to appear.

Bailiff - An attendant of the court.

Battery - The unlawful application of force to the person of another.

Bench - The court and the judges composing the court collectively.

Bench Warrant - An order of the court empowering the police or other legal authority to seize a person.

Bias Incident - A crime caused by the criminal's animosity towards the victim's race, religion, ethnicity, or sexual orientation; a hate crime.

Bill of Rights - The first eight amendments to the United States Constitution.

Burden of Proof - The duty of a party to substantiate an allegation or issue to convince the trier of fact as to the truth of their claim.

Capacity - Capacity is the legal qualification concerning the ability of one to understand the nature and effects of one's acts.

Capital Crime - A crime for which the death penalty may, but need not necessarily, be imposed.

Capital Punishment - The penalty of death.

Circumstantial Evidence - Indirect evidence by which a principal fact may be inferred.

Concerted Action - An act which is planned and carried out between parties who are acting together.

Conclusive Evidence - Evidence which is incontrovertible.

Concurrent - In criminal law, refers to sentences which are to be served simultaneously.

GLOSSARY

Confession - In criminal law, an admission of guilt or other incriminating statement made by the accused.

Confidence Game - A scheme where the perpetrator wins the confidence of his or her victim in order to cheat the victim out of a sum of money or other valuable.

Confrontation Clause - A Sixth Amendment right of the Constitution which permits the accused in a criminal prosecution to confront the witness against him.

Consecutive - In criminal law, refers to sentences which are to be served in numerical order.

Consent Search - A search which is carried out with the voluntary authorization of the subject of the search.

Conspiracy - A scheme by two or more persons to commit a criminal or unlawful act.

Conspirator - One of the parties involved in a conspiracy.

Constitution - The fundamental principles of law which frame a governmental system.

Constitutional Right - Refers to the individual liberties granted by the constitution of a state or the federal government.

Court - The branch of government responsible for the resolution of disputes arising under the laws of the government.

Criminal Court - The court designed to hear prosecutions under the criminal laws.

Cross-Examination - The questioning of a witness by someone other than the one who called the witness to the stand concerning matters about which the witness testified during direct examination.

Cruel and Unusual Punishment - Refers to punishment that is shocking to the ordinary person, inherently unfair, or excessive in comparison to the crime committed.

District Attorney - An officer of a governmental body with the duty to prosecute those accused of crimes.

Docket - A list of cases on the court's calendar.

Double Jeopardy - Fifth Amendment provision providing that an individual shall not be subject to prosecution for the same offense more than one time.

Due Process Rights - All rights which are of such fundamental importance as to require compliance with due process standards of fairness and justice.

Entrapment - In criminal law, refers to the use of trickery by the police to induce the defendant to commit a crime for which he or she has a predisposition to commit.

Exclusionary Rule - A constitutional rule of law providing that evidence procured by illegal police conduct, although otherwise admissible, will be excluded at trial.

Eyewitness - A person who can testify about a matter because of his or her own presence at the time of the event.

Fact Finder - In a judicial or administrative proceeding, the person, or group of persons, that has the responsibility of determining the acts relevant to decide a controversy.

Fact Finding - A process by which parties present their evidence and make their arguments to a neutral person, who issues a nonbinding report based on the findings, which usually contains a recommendation for settlement.

Felony - A crime of a graver or more serious nature than those designated as misdemeanors.

Felony Murder - A first degree murder charge which results when a homicide occurs during the course of certain specified felonies, such as arson and robbery.

Fine - A financial penalty imposed upon a defendant.

Forfeiture - The loss of goods or chattels, as a punishment for some crime or misdemeanor of the party forfeiting, and as a compensation for the offense and injury committed against the one to whom they are forfeited.

Fraud - A false representation of a matter of fact, whether by words or by conduct, by false or misleading allegations, or by concealment of that which should have been disclosed.

GLOSSARY

Hearing - A proceeding to determine an issue of fact based on the evidence presented.

Hearsay Rule - The evidence rule that declares any statement, other than that by a witness who is testifying at the hearing, is not admissible as evidence to prove the truth of the matter asserted, unless it falls under an exception to the rule.

Homicide - The killing of a human being by another human being.

Hung Jury - A jury which cannot render a verdict because its members cannot reconcile their differences to a necessary standard, e.g. unanimity, substantial majority.

Illegal - Against the law.

Immunity - A benefit of exemption from a duty or penalty.

Impaneling - Selecting and swearing in a panel of jurors for duty.

Imprisonment - The confinement of an individual, usually as punishment for a crime.

Indictment - A formal written accusation of criminal charges submitted to a grand jury for investigation and indorsement.

Information - A written accusation of a crime submitted by the prosecutor to inform the accused and the court of the charges and the facts of the crime.

Injury - Any damage done to another's person, rights, reputation or property.

Jail - Place of confinement where a person in custody of the government awaits trial or serves a sentence after conviction.

Jailhouse Lawyer - An inmate who gains knowledge of the law through self-study, and assists fellow inmates in preparation of appeals, although he or she is not licensed to practice law.

Judge - The individual who presides over a court, and whose function it is to determine controversies.

Jury - A group of individuals summoned to decide the facts in issue in a lawsuit.

Jury Trial - A trial during which the evidence is presented to a jury so that they can determine the issues of fact, and render a verdict based upon the law as it applies to their findings of fact.

Larceny - The unlawful taking of the property of another, without his or her consent, with the intention of converting it to one's own use.

Legal Aid - A national organization established to provide legal services to those who are unable to afford private representation.

Lineup - A police procedure whereby a suspect is placed in line with other persons of similar description so that a witness to the crime may attempt an identification.

Malice - A state of mind that accompanies the intentional commission of a wrongful act.

Manslaughter - The unlawful taking of another's life without malice aforethought.

Mens Rea - A guilty mind.

Misdemeanor - Criminal offenses which are less serious than felonies and carry lesser penalties.

Mistrial - A trial which is terminated prior to the return of a verdict, such as occurs when the jury is unable to reach a verdict.

Modus Operandi - Latin for "the manner of operation." Refers to the characteristic method used by a criminal in carrying out his or her actions.

Nolo Contendere - Latin for "I do not wish to contend." Statement by a defendant who does not wish to contest a charge. Although tantamount to a plea of guilty for the offense charged, it cannot be used against the defendant in another forum.

Not Guilty - The plea of a defendant in a criminal action denying the offense with which he or she is charged.

Obstruction of Justice - An offense by which one hinders the process by which individuals seek justice in the court, such as by intimidating jury members.

Offense - Any misdemeanor or felony violation of the law for which a penalty is prescribed.

GLOSSARY

Pardon - To release from further punishment, either conditionally or unconditionally.

Parole - The conditional release from imprisonment whereby the convicted individual serves the remainder of his or her sentence outside of prison as long as he or she is in compliance with the terms and conditions of parole.

Penal Institution - A place of confinement for convicted criminals.

Polygraph - A lie detector test.

Prejudice - A negative belief about a group of people who share a common characteristic, e.g. a particular race or religion.

Presumption of Innocence - In criminal law, refers to the doctrine that an individual is considered innocent of a crime until he or she is proven guilty.

Prisoner - One who is confined to a prison or other penal institution for the purpose of awaiting trial for a crime, or serving a sentence after conviction of a crime.

Probable Cause - The standard which must be met in order for there to be a valid search and seizure or arrest. It includes the showing of facts and circumstances reasonably sufficient and credible to permit the police to obtain a warrant.

Prosecution - The process of pursuing a civil lawsuit or a criminal trial.

Prosecutor - The individual who prepares a criminal case against an individual accused of a crime.

Public Defender - A lawyer hired by the government to represent an indigent person accused of a crime.

Racial Slur - A negative remark that demonstrates a racial prejudice.

Restitution - The act of making an aggrieved party whole by compensating him or her for any loss or damage sustained.

Robbery - The felonious act of stealing from a person, by the use of force or the threat of force, so as to put the victim in fear.

Search and Seizure - The search by law enforcement officials of a person or place in order to seize evidence to be used in the investigation and prosecution of a crime.

Search Warrant - A judicial order authorizing and directing law enforcement officials to search a specified location for specific items or individuals.

Self-Defense - The right to protect oneself, one's family, and one's property from an aggressor.

Sentence - The punishment given a convicted criminal by the court.

Subpoena - A court issued document compelling the appearance of a witness before the court.

Summons - A mandate requiring the appearance of the defendant in an action under penalty of having judgment entered against him for failure to do so.

Suppression of Evidence - The refusal to produce or permit evidence for use in litigation, such as when there has been an illegal search and seizure of the evidence.

Suspended Sentence - A sentence which is not executed contingent upon the defendant's observance of certain court-order terms and conditions.

Taking the Fifth - The term given to an individual's right not to incriminate oneself under the Fifth Amendment.

Testify - The offering of a statement in a judicial proceeding, under oath and subject to the penalty of perjury.

Testimony - The sworn statement make by a witness in a judicial proceeding.

Transferred Intent - The doctrine which provides that if a defendant intends harm to A, but harms B instead, the intent is deemed transferred to B, as far as the defendant's liability to B in tort is concerned.

Unreasonable Search and Seizure - A search and seizure which has not met the constitutional requirements under the Fourth and Fourteenth Amendment.

Verdict - The definitive answer given by the jury to the court concerning the matters of fact committed to the jury for their deliberation and determination.

Warrant - An official order directing that a certain act be undertaken, such as an arrest.

Warrantless Arrest - An arrest carried out without a warrant.

GLOSSARY

White Collar Crime - Refers to a class of non-violent offenses which have their basis in fraud and dishonesty.

Wrongful Death Statute - A statute that creates a cause of action for any wrongful act, neglect, or default that causes death.

BIBLIOGRAPHY AND ADDITIONAL READING

BIBLIOGRAPHY

Black's Law Dictionary, Fifth Edition. St. Paul, MN: West Publishing Company, 1979.

Ginsburg, William L. *Victims' Rights: The Complete Guide to Crime Victim Compensation.* Clearwater, FL: Sphinx Publishing, 1994.

Lurigio, Arthur J., Skogan, Wesley G., Davis, Robert C. *Victims of Crime: Problems, Policies, and Programs.* Newbury Park, CA: Sage Publications, 1990.

Poliny, Valiant R.W. *A Public Policy Analysis of the Emerging Victims Rights Movement.* Bethesda, MD: Austin & Winfield, 1994.

Sank, Diane, and Caplan, David I. *To Be A Victim: Encounters with Crime and Injustice.* New York, NY: Plenum Press, 1991.

Viano, Emilio C. *The Victimology Handbook.* New York, NY: Garland Publications, 1990.

344.7303288 JAS
Jasper, Margaret C.
Victim's rights law /

DISCARD